For Mental Arithmetic practice, it has to be CGP!

There's no better way to improve Mental Arithmetic skills
than with practice, and this incredible CGP Question Book
is packed with the best practice around.

There are stacks of questions tailored to Year 6 pupils, plus Listening Tests
with online audio to help develop their listening skills. We've also added
regular Progress Tests to keep track of how pupils are doing.

And of course, the answers to every question
are available online. You're welcome!

What CGP is all about

Our sole aim here at CGP is to produce the highest quality
books — carefully written, immaculately presented and
dangerously close to being funny.

Then we work our socks off to get them out to you
— at the cheapest possible prices.

Contents

The answers to every question in the book are available online — to find them, scan the QR code on the left with your smartphone or go to cgpbooks.co.uk/MA-Year6.

You'll find links to all of the audio files for the Listening Tests there, too — amazing!

Published by CGP

Editors: Martha Bozic, Abigail Brindley, Sarah George, David Ryan and Caley Simpson.

With thanks to Alison Griffin and Glenn Rogers for the proofreading.

With thanks to Jade Sim for the copyright research.

ISBN: 978 1 83774 042 0

Printed by Zenith Print & Packaging Ltd, Pontypridd.
Clipart from Corel®

Based on the classic CGP style created by Richard Parsons.

Text, design, layout and original illustrations © Coordination Group Publications Ltd. (CGP) 2023 All rights reserved.

Photocopying this book is not permitted, even if you have a CLA licence.
Extra copies are available from CGP with next day delivery • 0800 1712 712 • www.cgpbooks.co.uk

About this Book

This book is split into **three sections**. Each section contains mixed tests covering a range of Year 6 Maths topics. You should aim to do all your working **in your head**, without writing anything down.

36

Test 6

Warm Up Questions

Three out of every seven animals on a farm are sheep. There are 240 sheep on the farm.

1) What is the ratio of sheep to other animals on the farm in its simplest form?

2) How many animals on the farm aren't sheep?

Part A

1. What is 3.79 ÷ 10? ....
2. How many hours are in 1.5 days? .... hours
3. What is 9650 – 4080? ....
4. Work out $\frac{5}{6} \times \frac{1}{10}$, giving your answer in its simplest form. ....
5. Liz cycles 32 km. Approximately how many miles does she cycle? Use the conversion 5 miles ≈ 8 km. .... miles
6. What is the size of angle m? ....°
7. A cafe sells cups of tea for £1 and cookies for £1.50. How much money do they get in total from 70 cups of tea and 100 cookies? £..................
8. What is 7 × 250? ....

Part B

14. What is $\frac{64}{400}$ as a decimal? ....
15. A sequence has the rule "subtract 4 from the previous term". The third term is 7. What is the first term? ....
16. Find the smallest number that is a multiple of 4, 10 and 25. ....
17. What is the size of angle k? ....°
18. The distance around the Sun is 4 378 993 km. Round this to the nearest hundred thousand km. .... km
19. A cuboid box has a volume of 120 cm³. It is 10 cm long and 3 cm tall. What is the width of the box? .... cm
20. $\frac{1}{4}$ of pupils in Rina's class have a dog. 6 pupils have a dog. How many pupils are in Rina's class? ....

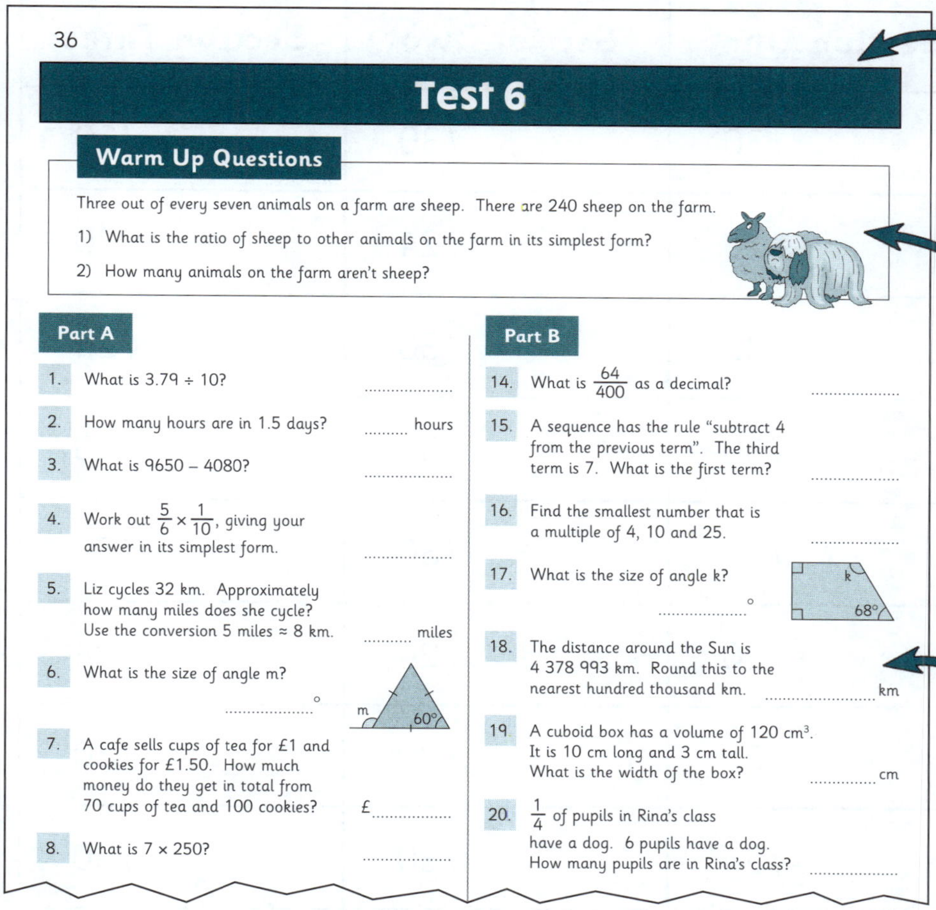

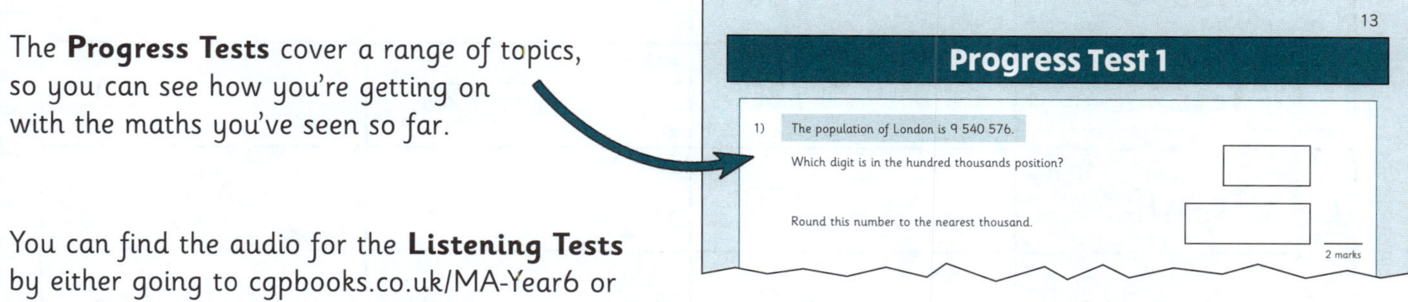

The tests get **trickier** between the sections — the Section 1 tests are easier and the Section 3 tests are a bit harder.

Some tests have **Warm Up Questions** to help get your brain in gear, before you tackle the rest of the questions.

Each test is in **two parts**, so you don't have to do all the questions in the test at once.

There is also a **Progress Test** and three **Listening Tests** at the end of each section. These are the same level of difficulty as the rest of the tests in that section.

The **Progress Tests** cover a range of topics, so you can see how you're getting on with the maths you've seen so far.

13

Progress Test 1

1) The population of London is 9 540 576.

Which digit is in the hundred thousands position?

Round this number to the nearest thousand.

2 marks

You can find the audio for the **Listening Tests** by either going to cgpbooks.co.uk/MA-Year6 or by scanning the QR code at the top of each Listening Test page.

You will hear each question twice, and then you will have 5 or 10 seconds to answer it.

Listening Test 1

1. ....
2. .... %
3. ....
4. ....
5. ....
6. .... ml
7. ....
8. £..................
9. ....
10. ....

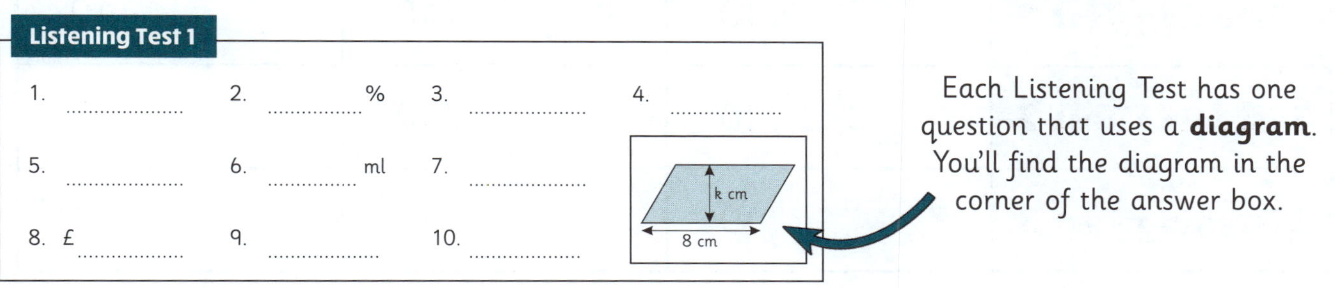

Each Listening Test has one question that uses a **diagram**. You'll find the diagram in the corner of the answer box.

Progress Chart

Use this chart to keep track of your scores in each test.

	Section One	Section Two	Section Three
Test 1	/30	/30	/30
Test 2	/26	/24	/30
Test 3	/30	/30	/24
Test 4	/30	/30	/30
Test 5	/26	/30	/30
Test 6	/30	/24	/24
Test 7	/30	/30	/30
Test 8	/24	/30	/30
Test 9	/30	/24	/30
Test 10	/30	/30	/24
Test 11	/30	/24	/30
Test 12	/30	/30	
Progress Test	/17	/14	/15
Listening Test 1	/10	/10	/10
Listening Test 2	/10	/10	/10
Listening Test 3	/10	/10	/10

Test 1

Part A

1. What is 140 + 235? ....

2. What is the next term in the sequence 7, 11, 15, 19, ...? ....

3. What is 3.7 litres + 400 ml in ml? .... ml

4. Which digit in 6 723 489 is in the millions position? ....

5. Which of the numbers below doesn't have 9 as a factor?

| 27 | 54 | 108 | 63 | 71 |

....

6. What is 1200 m in kilometres? .... km

7. Karim has 30 books. He buys 10 more, then shares all of his books equally between 5 shelves. How many books are on each shelf? ....

8. Work out the size of angle a in this triangle.

.... ° 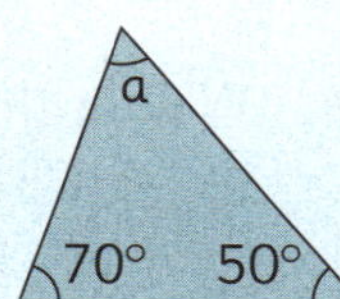

9. What is 273 568 rounded to the nearest hundred? ....

10. Write $\frac{10}{40}$ in its simplest form. ....

11. Which digit is in the hundreds place after 2.7 is multiplied by 1000? ....

12. What are the common factors of 7 and 35? .... and ....

13. Daniel bakes 25 cookies and eats 20% of them. Stef bakes 40 cookies and eats 10% of them. Who eats more cookies? ....

14. What is 462 ÷ 10? ....

15. Which of the following numbers isn't prime?

| 2 | 3 | 5 | 6 | 7 | 11 |

....

Part B

16. Which is bigger: $\frac{10}{50}$ or 25%? ....

17. What is 2910 − 400? ....

18. The base of a triangle is 4 cm long and its vertical height is 3 cm. What is the area of the triangle? .... cm²

19. What is 80 × 7? ....

20. A supermarket sells bananas in bags of 7. Sue buys 4 bags of bananas. Amie buys 2 bags of bananas. How many bananas do they have altogether? ....

21. What is $\frac{1}{3}$ ÷ 3? ....

22. Write 2 : 4 in its simplest form. ....

23. Peter jogs for 45 minutes, then swims for 1 hour and 15 minutes. How long does he exercise for in hours? .... hours 

24. What is $\frac{1}{15}$ + $\frac{1}{5}$? ....

25. What is 1420 g in kilograms? .... kg

26. Which of these fractions is the biggest?

| $\frac{1}{2}$ | $\frac{2}{3}$ | $\frac{3}{6}$ |

....

27. What is 550 ÷ 11? ....

28. Use this graph to convert £5 to Japanese yen.

.... yen

29. Which number between 1 and 50 is a common multiple of 5 and 8? ....

30. x + 10 = 18 What is the value of x? ....

© CGP — not to be photocopied

Test 2

Warm Up Questions

Look at this coordinate grid. What are the new coordinates of point A when the shape is:

1) reflected in the x-axis?

2) translated 3 units to the left and 3 units down?

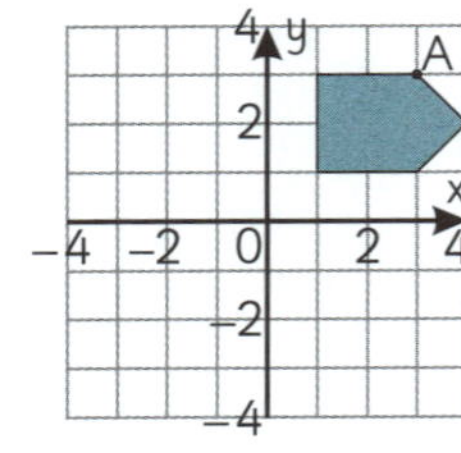

Part A

1. What is 21.93 × 100? ....

2. Which digit is in the ten thousands position of 76 010? ....

3. Write 75% as a fraction in its simplest form. ....

4. A rectangle is 15 cm long and 3 cm wide. What is its area? .... cm²

5. What is 680 + 130? ....

6. Alan has two barrels. One can hold 7200 ml of liquid, and the other can hold 3.7 litres. What is the difference between their capacities in ml? .... ml

7. What is $\frac{1}{4} \div 2$? ....

8. What is 1781 − 241? ....

9. What is the next term in the sequence? −17, −12, −7, −2, ...

10. Which of the numbers below doesn't have 6 as a factor?

   | 18 | 60 | 36 | 46 |

   ....

11. Ed runs laps of a park that has a perimeter of 500 m. How many laps does he need to do to run 5 km? ....

12. Find the area of this triangle.

   .... cm²

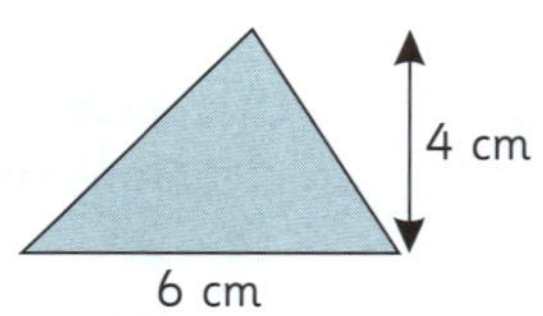

13. What is $\frac{1}{6} + \frac{5}{18}$ in its simplest form? ....

Part B

14. Which of these fractions cannot be simplified to make its denominator 4?

   | $\frac{15}{20}$ | $\frac{2}{16}$ | $\frac{10}{40}$ |

   ....

15. What is 40% of 60? ....

16. Glen scores 507 308 points at an arcade. What is his score rounded to the nearest thousand? ....

17. What is 210 ÷ 3? ....

18. What is the next prime number after 7? ....

19. What is 1.56 kg + 340 g in kg? .... kg

20. What is 3.27 ÷ 10? ....

21. This pie chart shows the colours of cars in a car park. There are 160 cars in total. How many are white?

   ....

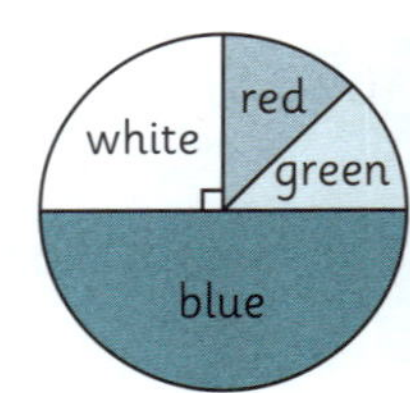

22. Which is lighter? A: 20% of 10 kg or B: 25% of 12 kg? ....

23. What is $\frac{10}{16}$ in its simplest form? ....

24. Which symbol (<, > or =) goes in the box below to make this statement correct?

   4 927 834 [?] 4 928 834 ....

25. What is 120 × 5? ....

26. R = 7e. What is the value of R when e = 4? ....

© CGP — not to be photocopied

Test 3

Part A

1.   What is 3 × 300? ....

2.   Round 7 794 456 to the nearest hundred thousand. ....

3.   Which is smaller: 75% or $\frac{10}{16}$? ....

4.   How many factors does 40 have? ....

5.   What is 465 ÷ 100? ....

6.   Clare has 130 beads. She uses them to make 5 identical necklaces. How many beads are on each necklace? ....

7.   What is 10% of 7.5 kg? .... kg

8.   What is $\frac{18}{60}$ in its simplest form? ....

9.   40 hot drinks were made in a staff room. 40% were cups of tea. How many cups of tea were made? ....

10.   Which digit is in the ten thousands position of 378 216? ....

11.   Work out the size of angle v.

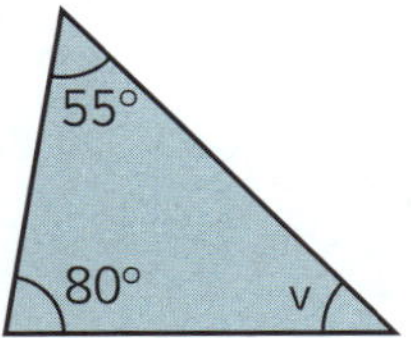

.... °

12.   What is 191 × 10? ....

13.   9 games cost £270. Each game costs the same amount. How much does one game cost? £ ....

14.   c − 2 = 17
What is the value of c? ....

15.   There are 60 seeds in a packet. Alice plants 4 packets of seeds. 150 of the seeds grow. How many seeds don't grow? ....

16.   Write 16 : 4 in its simplest form. ....

Part B

17.   Harriet cycled 900 m yesterday. Today she cycled 1.3 km. How far did she cycle in total? .... km

18.   What is $\frac{3}{10} + \frac{13}{20}$? ....

19.   Find the next term in this sequence:
26, 22, 18, 14, ...

20.   Find the area of this rectangle.

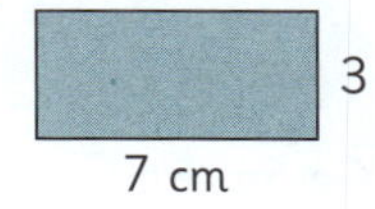

.... cm²

21.   After 4932 is divided by 100, which digit is in the tens place? ....

22.   What is $\frac{1}{3} \div 2$? ....

23.   Will plays a video game. He scores 134 points on level one and 664 points on level two. How many points does he score in total? ....

24.   What is 472 − 290? ....

25.   The base of a triangle is 3 cm long and its vertical height is 30 cm. What is the area of the triangle? .... cm²

26.   What is 4950 ml in litres? l

27.   It took Shivana 2.5 hours to run a half-marathon. How long did it take her in minutes? .... mins

28.   Which of these fractions is the smallest?

$\frac{8}{12}$	$\frac{9}{15}$	$\frac{11}{22}$

....

29.   Which number between 3 and 7 is prime? ....

30.   Point X has coordinates (2, 5). It is translated 3 units to the right and 3 units up. What are the new coordinates of point X? ....

© CGP — not to be photocopied   Section One

Test 4

Part A

1. What is 3.82 × 1000? ....

2. What is the value of the 7 in 175 111? ....

3. What is 1225 + 610? ....

4. How many factors does 28 have? ....

5. There are 101 tents on a campsite. Each tent has 7 tent pegs. How many tent pegs are there altogether? ....

6. A bag of rice weighs 3500 g. Kieran uses 750 g to make rice pudding. How much does the bag of rice weigh now? .... g

7. What is $\frac{7}{21}$ in its simplest form? ....

8. Caleb buys 12 stamps that cost 40p each. How much does he spend in pounds? £ ....

9. Round 63 849 to the nearest hundred. ....

10. What is 180 minutes in hours? .... hours

11. Marcus bakes 50 cupcakes. He eats 5 of them, then shares the rest equally between 5 people. How many does each person get? ....

12. What is 80% as a fraction in its simplest form? ....

13. Find the area of this rectangle.

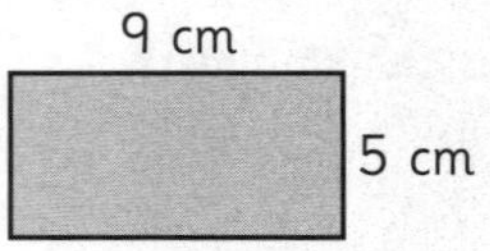

9 cm

5 cm

.... cm²

14. Which digit is in the thousands position of 120 974? ....

15. What is 600 ÷ 5? ....

16. What is the radius of a circle with a diameter of 8 m? .... m

Part B

17. What is 9.213 kg in grams? .... g

18. The pie chart shows breakfast choices of guests in a hotel. There are 120 guests. How many choose cereal?

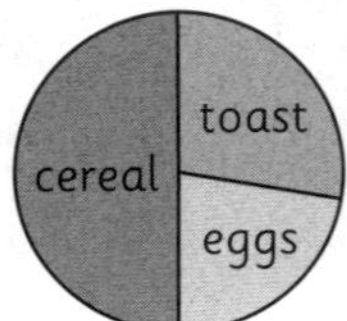

....

19. What is $\frac{3}{4} - \frac{1}{2}$ in its simplest form? ....

20. What is 5 litres − 1200 ml in litres? l

21. A box of crayons weighs 63.3 g. There are 10 identical crayons in a box. How much does one crayon weigh? .... g

22. Which of these fractions cannot be simplified to make its denominator 3?

$\frac{3}{9}$ $\frac{20}{30}$ $\frac{3}{6}$

....

23. What is the smallest number that is a multiple of both 10 and 12? ....

24. What is $\frac{1}{6} \div 3$? ....

25. Find the next term in this sequence: 67, 56, 45, 34, ...

26. A squirrel has 40 acorns. It stores 90% of them for winter. How many acorns does the squirrel store? ....

27. Write 8 : 2 in its simplest form. ....

28. Which of these numbers is prime?

4 9 12 13 15

....

29. The base of a triangle is 12 cm and its vertical height is 4 cm. What is the area of the triangle? .... cm²

30. Look at the formula t = 8n. What is the value of t when n = 6? ....

© CGP — not to be photocopied

Test 5

Warm Up Questions

This graph shows how much a sunflower grew over 10 weeks.

1) How tall was the sunflower after 3 weeks?

2) How many weeks did it take for the sunflower to reach 90 cm tall?

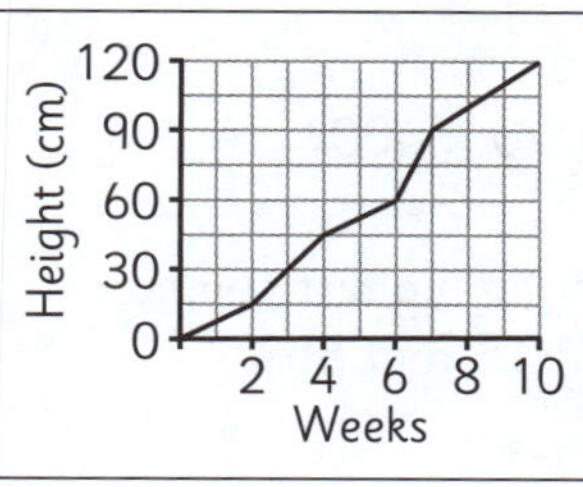

Part A

1. Find the missing term in the sequence.
60, [?], 50, 45, 40 ....

2. Look at the number on the cards below.

| 4 | 8 | 7 | 6 | 2 | 9 | 4 |

What new number is made by swapping the thousands and tens digits? ....

3. What is $912 \div 10$? ....

4. How many common factors do 27 and 36 have? ....

5. What is $210 + 670$? ....

6. There are 30 pupils in a class. 70% of them have brown hair. How many pupils have brown hair? ....

7. What is $8689 - 3120$? ....

8. What is $\frac{15}{25}$ in its simplest form? ....

9. Anita sleeps for 7.5 hours. She goes back to sleep for another 30 minutes. How many hours did she sleep for? .... hours

10. What is 0.087×1000? ....

11. Which of these fractions is the smallest?

$$\frac{2}{4} \quad \frac{2}{6} \quad \frac{2}{3}$$

....

12. Round 7 708 791 to the nearest ten thousand. ....

13. What is 295 ml in litres? l

Part B

14. Joe has half a pizza. He shares it equally between 4 people. What fraction of the whole pizza does each person get? ....

15. What is $720 \div 8$? ....

16. How many prime numbers are there between 10 and 20? ....

17. Which is bigger: $\frac{1}{3}$ or 20%? ....

18. Each side of a square is 7 cm long. What is the area of the square? .... cm²

19. A dog weighs 50 kg and a cat weighs 3200 g. What is the total weight of both animals in kg? .... kg

20. $x + 3 = 13$
What is the value of x? ....

21. What number between 60 and 80 is a common multiple of 5 and 7? ....

22. What is $\frac{2}{3} - \frac{2}{9}$ in its simplest form? ....

23. What is 3500 m − 1.45 km in metres? .... m

24. Find the area of this triangle.

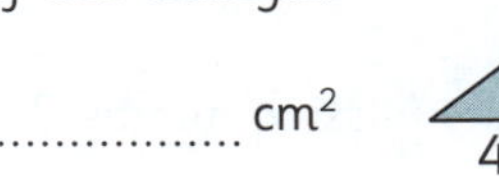

.... cm²

25. What is 230×3? ....

26. Point A has coordinates (1, 3). It is translated 4 units to the right and 2 units up. What are the new coordinates of point A? ....

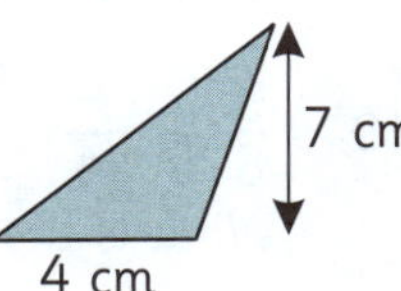

© CGP — not to be photocopied

Test 6

Part A

1. What is 20×400? ....

2. What is the highest common factor of 15 and 55? ....

3. What is the value of the 2 in 1 234 567? ....

4. What is $892 \div 1000$? ....

5. Which of the numbers below is a common multiple of 5 and 12?

| 45 | 35 | 30 | 60 | 52 |

....

6. Round 46 213 to the nearest thousand. ....

7. What is 30% as a decimal? ....

8. There are 80 people on a bus. 20% of them are standing. How many people are standing? ....

9. What is $1080 \div 90$? ....

10. There are 4520 ants in an ant farm. 313 of them escape. How many ants are left? ....

11. Find the area of this triangle.

2 m
2 m
.... m^2

12. Which digit in 8 093 241 is in the hundred thousands position? ....

13. $\dfrac{3}{8} = \dfrac{?}{24}$
What is the missing number? ....

14. Asim puts £10 into a piggy bank every day. How many weeks does it take him to save £210? .... weeks

15. What is the diameter of a circle with a radius of 10 cm? .... cm

Part B

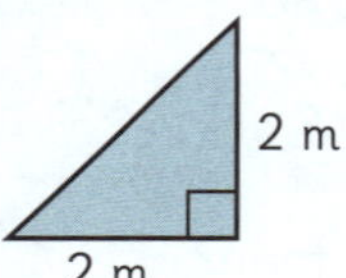

16. 25 strawberries and 15 raspberries are used to make one jar of jam. Kara uses 400 berries in total. How many jars of jam does she make? ....

17. What is $\dfrac{3}{15}$ in its simplest form? ....

18. An egg weighs 64 g. How much does the egg weigh in kg? .... kg

19. This pie chart shows the types of sandwiches sold at a cafe. They sold 12 cheese sandwiches. How many egg sandwiches did they sell?

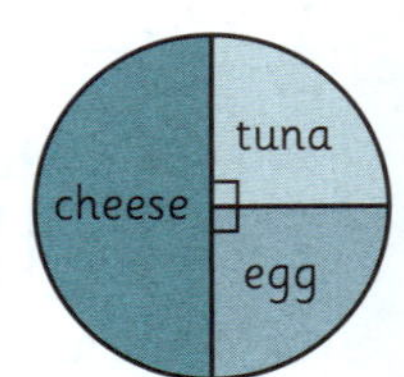

....

20. What is $\dfrac{1}{4} - \dfrac{1}{12}$ in its simplest form? ....

21. A rectangle is 5 cm wide and 6 cm long. What is the area of the rectangle? .... cm^2

22. What is $476 + 324$? ....

23. It took Mae 0.75 hours to cook a meal. How long did it take her in minutes? .... mins

24. What is 630 ml + 4.3 litres in ml? .... ml

25. What is $\dfrac{1}{2} \div 5$? ....

26. There are 60 guests at a party. 15 leave and 26 more arrive. How many guests are at the party now? ....

27. Write $3 : 9$ in its simplest form. ....

28. What is the next term in the sequence 3, 10, 17, 24, ...? ....

29. What is the size of angle a?

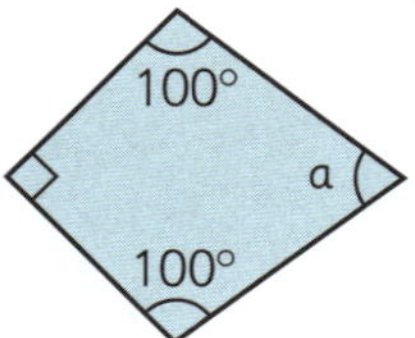

.... °

30. $q + 2 = 12$
What is the value of q? ....

© CGP — not to be photocopied

Test 7

Part A

1. Which digit is in the millions position of 9 093 365? ....

2. What is $\frac{4}{12}$ in its simplest form? ....

3. Find the area of this rectangle.

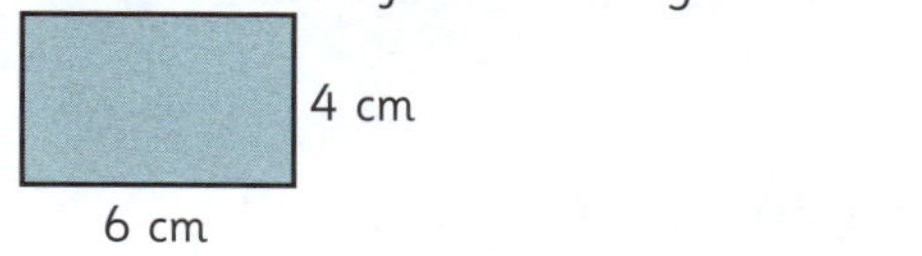

.... cm^2

4. Frankie runs 9.99 km. How far does she run in metres? .... m

5. What is 532 + 230? ....

6. What number between 30 and 50 is a common multiple of 5 and 8? ....

7. Which is smaller: $\frac{3}{20}$ or 10%? ....

8. There are 44 people in a train carriage. 50% of them are reading. How many people are reading? ....

9. What is the value of the 6 in 30 699? ....

10. What is $\frac{1}{5} \div 3$? ....

11. What is 0.35 × 1000? ....

12. A crate of potatoes weighs 5000 g. Hassan uses 2.3 kg of them. How much does the crate weigh now, in grams? .... g

13. What is 240 minutes in hours? .... hours

14. What is the area of this triangle?

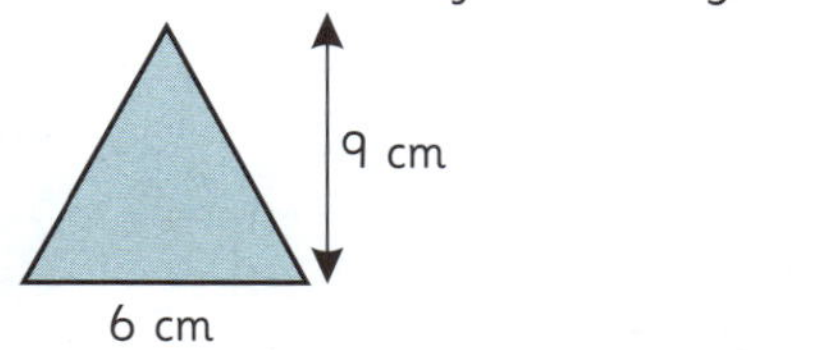

.... cm^2

15. Which of these numbers is not prime?

7 5 11 3 12

....

16. What is 60% of 15? ....

Part B

17. What is $\frac{2}{3} - \frac{1}{6}$ in its simplest form? ....

18. A city has a population of 3 107 456. Round this to the nearest ten thousand. ....

19. Find the missing term in the sequence 95, ? , 75, 65, 55, ...

20. What is 33.1 ÷ 100? ....

21. Which of the following numbers is not a common factor of 12 and 54?

2 3 4 6

....

22. What is 350 × 4? ....

23. A potion uses 5 leaves. A wizard gathers 60 leaves then makes 8 potions. How many leaves are left over? ....

24. 3u = 15 What is the value of u? ....

25. David pours 2200 ml of water into a bucket, then adds another 0.58 litres. How much water is in the bucket in litres? l

26. Which fraction is the biggest: $\frac{3}{8}$, $\frac{3}{4}$ or $\frac{3}{6}$? ....

27. Use this graph to convert 2 ounces into grams.

.... g

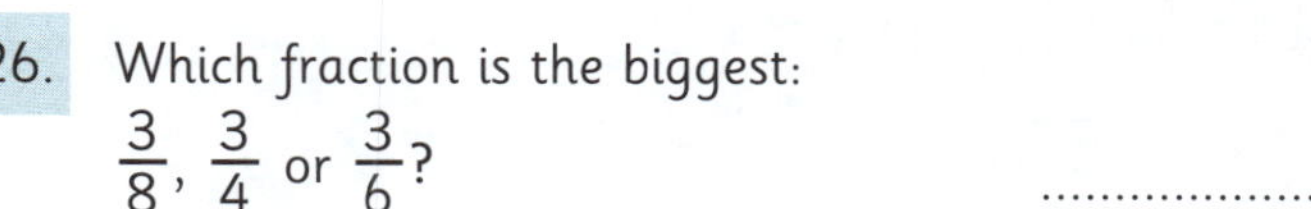

28. Point Y has coordinates (6, 1). It is translated 2 units to the left and 3 units down. What are the new coordinates of point Y? ....

29. What is 240 ÷ 30? ....

30. A bakery makes £876 in a day. They spend £139 on ingredients. How much do they have left over? £ ....

© CGP — not to be photocopied

Test 8

Warm Up Questions

1) A number has 7 millions, 8 hundred thousands, 3 thousands, 9 hundreds, 8 tens and 5 ones. What is this number in digits?

2) A number has 3 millions, 5 ten thousands, 2 thousands, 4 hundreds and 7 ones. What is this number in digits?

Part A

1. Which digit in 32 145 is in the thousands position? ....

2. What is 4356 + 400? ....

3. What is the next term in the sequence that begins 35, 29, 23, 17, ...? ....

4. Pinar has £257. She spends £135. How much does she have left? £ ....

5. Write $\frac{2}{4}$ in its simplest form. ....

6. A bowl of cake mixture weighs 2.2 kg. 900 g of flour is added. What is the total weight in kilograms? .... kg

7. What is 420 ÷ 7? ....

8. Find the area of this rectangle.

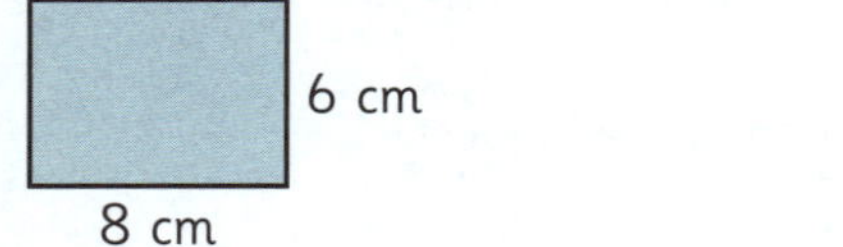

.... cm²

9. What is the diameter of a circle with a radius of 3 cm? .... cm

10. Which is bigger: $\frac{3}{4}$ or $\frac{7}{10}$? ....

11. There are 10 roses in a bunch. Karen picks enough roses to make 7 bunches, and has 3 roses left over. How many roses did she pick? ....

12. What is 4 × 500? ....

13. What is the smallest number that is a multiple of 3 and 6? ....

Part B

14. A crab has 10 legs. A group of crabs has 2130 legs between them. How many crabs are in the group? ....

15. What is $\frac{1}{2}$ ÷ 2? ....

16. Find the area of this triangle.

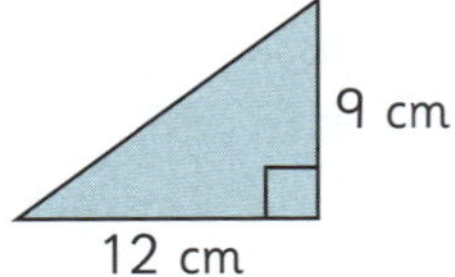

.... cm²

17. Round 931 273 to the nearest thousand. ....

18. What is 73.5 × 100? ....

19. What is $\frac{3}{8} + \frac{3}{16}$? ....

20. Bilal does two puzzles. One takes 1 hour 30 minutes and the other takes 50 minutes. How long does it take to do both puzzles? .... hours .... mins

21. Which of the numbers below is a multiple of both 3 and 7?

22 77 54 36 63

....

22. What is $\frac{3}{5}$ as a decimal? ....

23. Use the graph on the right to convert 20 pints to gallons.

.... gallons

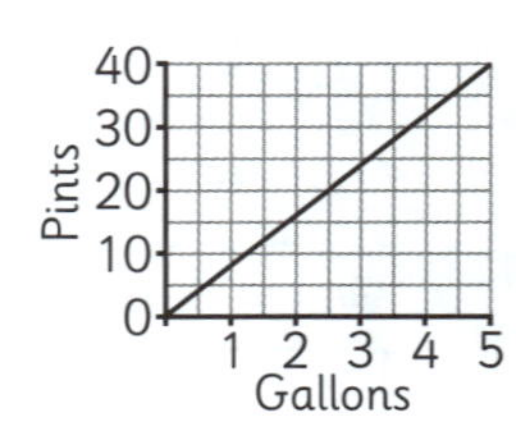

24. x − 3 = 7 What is the value of x? ....

  © CGP — not to be photocopied

Test 9

Part A

1. The population of Dentham is 152 450. Round this to the nearest hundred. ....

2. What is 8.26 × 10? ....

3. Maisam has 740 jelly beans and Liam has 260. How many do they have altogether? ....

4. What is 6850 m − 3.15 km in m? .... m

5. What is the value of the 4 in 98 847? ....

6. What is $\frac{16}{24}$ in its simplest form? ....

7. A jug holds 1000 ml of water when full. 3 full jugs of water are used to fill 15 identical cups. How much water is in each cup in millilitres? .... ml

8. What is 564 − 175? ....

9. What is $\frac{3}{4} \div 3$ in its simplest form? ....

10. Which of these numbers is not prime?

    | 17 | 23 | 13 | 21 | 19 |

    ....

11. Sinead watches a film for 1 hour and 50 minutes, then watches another for 90 minutes. How long does she spend watching the films in minutes? .... mins

12. What is 60 × 50? ....

13. What is the area of this rectangle?

    3 cm
    8 cm

    .... cm^2

14. Which number between 20 and 40 is a multiple of both 6 and 9? ....

15. What is 6.92 litres in millilitres? .... ml

16. What is the highest common factor of 8 and 16? ....

Part B

17. Ellie and Alex fence in 10 matches each. Ellie wins 60% of her matches and Alex wins $\frac{2}{5}$ of his. How many more matches does Ellie win? .... 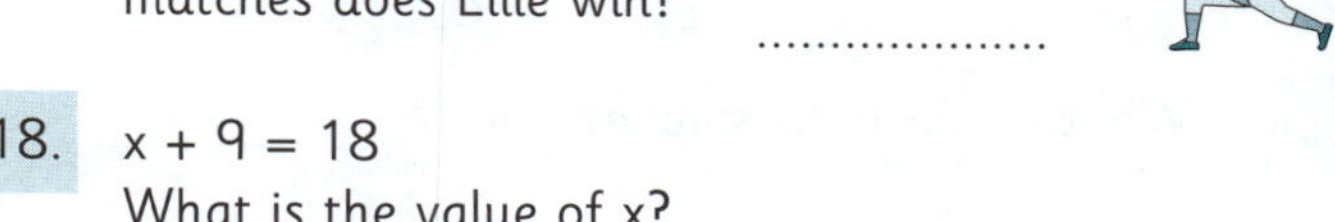

18. x + 9 = 18
    What is the value of x? ....

19. A sequence begins 3, 9, 15, ...
    What is the 5th term of the sequence? ....

20. What is the smallest number that is a multiple of both 6 and 8? ....

21. What is the size of angle c?

    c
    198°

    ....°

22. What is $\frac{1}{16} + \frac{1}{2}$? ....

23. Write 2 : 6 in its simplest form. ....

24. A triangle has a base of length 8 cm and a vertical height of 8 cm. What is the area of the triangle? .... cm^2

25. What is 1367 ÷ 100? ....

26. What is 2.45 kg in grams? .... g

27. Use the graph on the right to convert £4 into Chinese yuan.

    .... yuan

    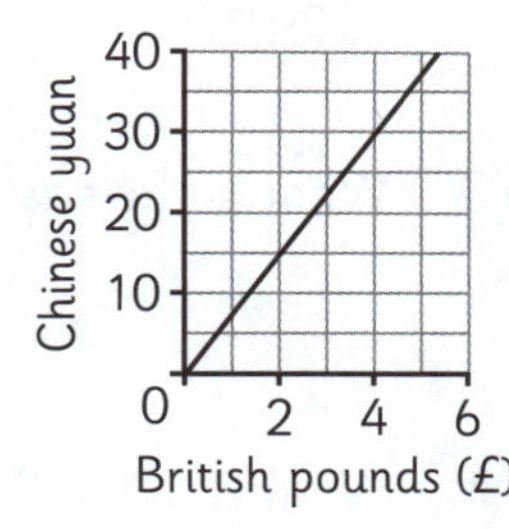

28. What is 189 ÷ 9? ....

29. Which of these fractions is the smallest?

    | $\frac{2}{12}$ | $\frac{4}{8}$ | $\frac{1}{4}$ |

    ....

30. Jake has 60 nails. He uses 75% of them to build a table. How many nails does he use? ....

© CGP — not to be photocopied Section One

Test 10

Part A

1. What is 0.24 × 100? ....

2. Round 8 897 816 to the nearest million. ....

3. What is $\frac{15}{20}$ in its simplest form? ....

4. What is the next term in the sequence 22, 25, 28, 31, ...? ....

5. Find the area of this triangle.

   .... cm^2

   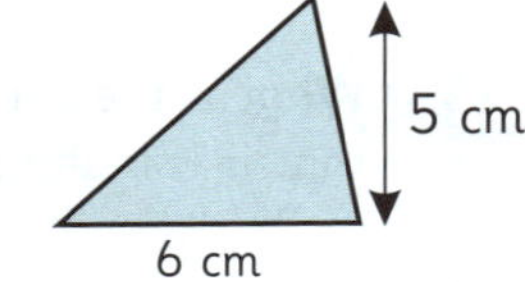

6. What is 360 ÷ 6? ....

7. What is the radius of a circle with a diameter of 16 cm? .... cm

8. Imran gets $\frac{7}{10}$ of the questions correct on a test. What is his score as a percentage? .... %

9. What is 821 + 151? ....

10. Which number between 25 and 45 is a common multiple of 4 and 10? ....

11. What is the value of the 9 in 29 100? ....

12. What is the size of angle b? .... °

    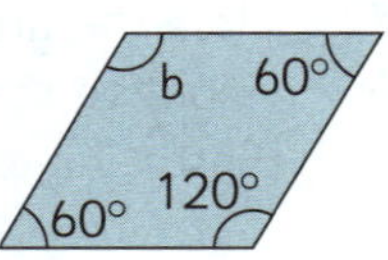

13. What is 12 340 ÷ 1000? ....

14. Which digit is in the tens place after 492 388 is divided by 1000? ....

15. What is $\frac{1}{6}$ ÷ 2? ....

16. Bonny cycles 6.25 km to the shop then 1.1 km to the park. How far does she cycle in metres? .... m

Part B

17. Write 9 : 12 in its simplest form. ....

18. $\frac{4}{5} = \frac{?}{30}$
    What is the missing number? ....

19. Lucy collects 40 shells. She sells 12 and splits the rest equally into 7 bags. How many shells are in each bag? ....

20. What is 10% of 99? ....

21. This pie chart shows types of tree in a forest. There are 440 trees in total. How many of them are birch?

    ....

    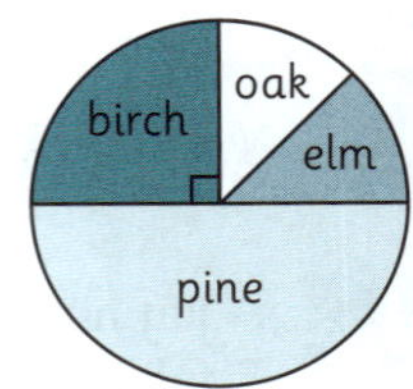

23. A rectangle is 20 cm long and 4 cm wide. What is the area of the rectangle? .... cm^2

22. What is 256 ml in litres? l

24. There are 700 chocolate chips in a bag. How many are there in 12 bags? ....

25. What is 2 hours – 25 minutes in minutes? .... mins

26. What is $\frac{1}{12} + \frac{2}{3}$ in its simplest form? ....

27. Look at the formula g = 4h. What is the value of h when g = 16? ....

28. Which of the following is not a common factor of 16 and 24?

    | 2 | 4 | 6 | 8 |

    ....

29. What is 3124 – 2111? ....

30. A bag of sugar weighs 2 kg. Carl uses 350 g to bake a cake. How much does the bag weigh now in kg?

    .... kg

© CGP — not to be photocopied

Test 11

Part A

1. What is the value of the 5 in 7 456 981? ....

2. What is the area of this rectangle?

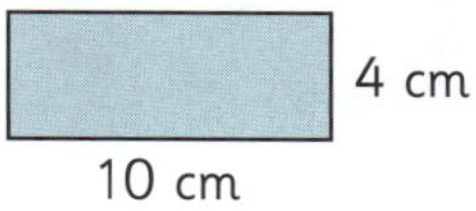

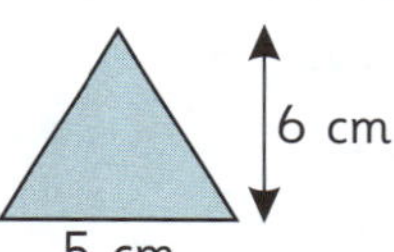

.... cm^2

3. Which digit is in the ones place after 3094 is divided by 1000? ....

4. 89 chocolates are shared equally between 12 boxes. How many chocolates are left over? ....

5. Round 4532 to the nearest hundred. ....

6. Taegan drank 1800 ml of water. How much did she drink in litres? l

7. What is the area of the triangle below?

.... cm^2

8. What is $\frac{1}{5} \div 4$? ....

9. Makala rowed her boat for 4.52 km. How far is this in metres? .... m

10. What is 375.2 × 10? ....

11. How many common factors do 6 and 12 have? ....

12. What is 0.2 as a percentage? .... %

13. James runs 685 m, then runs another 330 m. How far does he run in total? .... m

14. Which of these fractions is the smallest?

| $\frac{4}{6}$ | $\frac{5}{8}$ | $\frac{7}{12}$ |

....

15. What is 320 ÷ 4? ....

16. What is the size of angle a in the diagram below?

.... °

Part B

17. What is $\frac{1}{2} + \frac{3}{10}$ in its simplest form? ....

18. What is the next term in this sequence? −5, −2, 1, 4, ...

19. These cards show a 7-digit number.

| 7 | 6 | 3 | 4 | 5 | 9 | 0 |

What new number is made by swapping the tens and hundred thousands digits? ....

20. What is 60 × 30? ....

21. A snail crawls 30 cm. It then crawls another 1.2 m. How many cm does it travel in total?

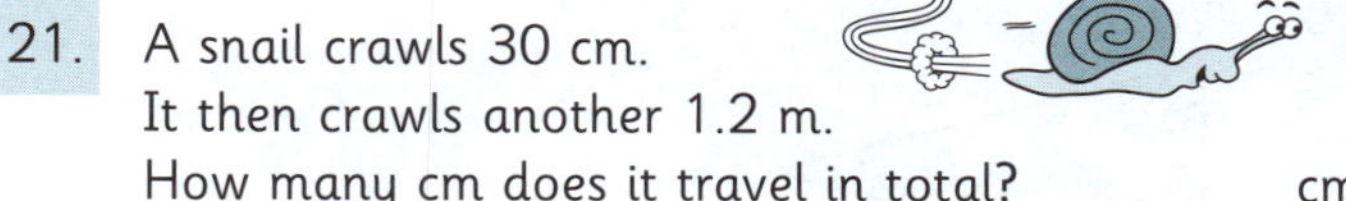

.... cm

22. Which is bigger: 0.8 or $\frac{1}{3}$? ....

23. Sandra has £200 and spends 50% of it. Raj has £300 and spends 30% of it. Who spends the most money? ....

24. Write 4 : 10 in its simplest form. ....

25. Which of these fractions can't be simplified?

| $\frac{4}{8}$ | $\frac{5}{15}$ | $\frac{9}{12}$ | $\frac{2}{7}$ | $\frac{4}{10}$ |

....

26. What is 9852 − 152? ....

27. This graph shows Sophie's heart rate while she is exercising. What is her heart rate after 5 minutes?

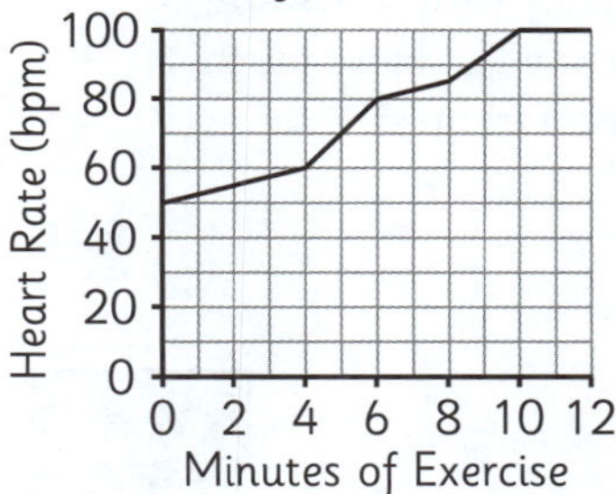

.... bpm

28. What is 300 minutes in hours? .... hours

29. x + 5 = 12
What is the value of x? ....

30. How many numbers between 1 and 6 are prime? ....

© CGP — not to be photocopied

Test 12

Part A

1. What is 4.6×100? ....

2. What is 3562 g in kilograms? .... kg

3. Round 147 398 to the nearest ten thousand. ....

4. What is the smallest number that is a multiple of 12 and 20? ....

5. What is $\frac{6}{24}$ in its simplest form? ....

6. What is the size of angle b?

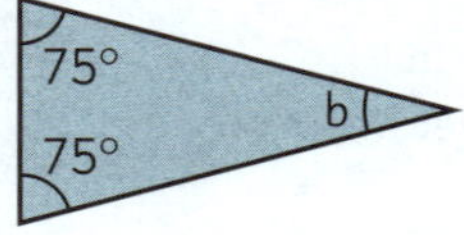

....................°

7. What is the value of the 3 in 3 808 950? ....

8. What is 80% of 20? ....

9. There are 6 wolves in a pack. There are 8 packs in the forest. 7 wolves leave the forest. How many wolves are left? ....

10. What is $\frac{1}{7} \div 2$? ....

11. What is $912 + 59$? ....

12. Ryan drinks 2 litres of water, 150 ml of juice and 200 ml of milk. How much does he drink in total in litres? l

13. What is $560 \div 7$? ....

14. Find the area of this rectangle. .... cm²

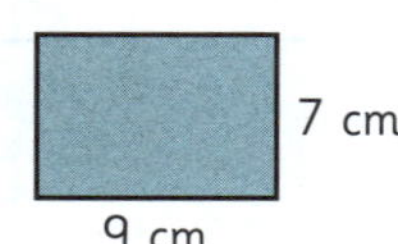

15. What is $\frac{4}{5}$ as a decimal? ....

16. 5678 people bought tickets to a concert, but 234 didn't go. How many people went to the concert? ....

Part B

17. Ivy has 20 stickers and gives 20% away. Bill has 30 stickers and gives 30% away. Who gives more stickers away? ....

18. How many common factors do 16 and 34 have? ....

19. What is the next prime number after 13? ....

20. How many minutes are in 3 hours 15 minutes? .... mins

21. A triangle has a base length of 11 cm and a vertical height of 2 cm. What is the area of the triangle? .... cm²

22. $x - 4 = 9$
What is the value of x? ....

23. What is $\frac{7}{9} - \frac{1}{3}$ in its simplest form? ....

24. What number is in the thousands position when 218 is multiplied by 100? ....

25. What is 120×70? ....

26. What is 42 m in kilometres? .... km

27. This graph shows how far Beth walked on a hike. How far had she walked after 3 hours?

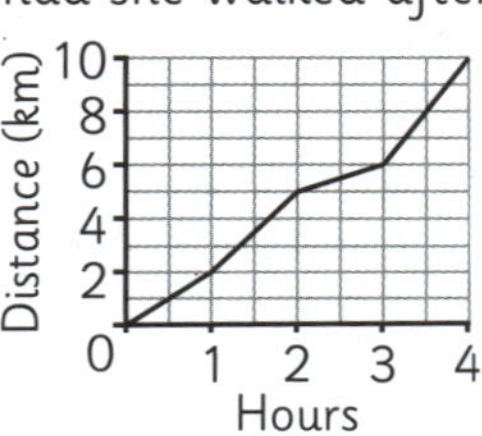

.... km

28. What is the next term in the sequence $-11, -6, -1, 4, \dots$? ....

29. What is $3451 \div 1000$? ....

30. $\frac{3}{15} = \frac{9}{?}$
What is the missing number? ....

© CGP — not to be photocopied

Section 1 Progress Test

1) The population of London is 9 540 576.

   Which digit is in the hundred thousands position?

   Round this number to the nearest thousand.

   2 marks

2) Richard grows a marrow that weighs 3240 g and a pumpkin that weighs 6.13 kg.

   What is the total weight of Richard's vegetables in kilograms?

   kg

   1 mark

3) There are 50 pupils on a school bus. 12 of them are wearing glasses.

   What fraction of the pupils on the bus are wearing glasses, in its simplest form?

   What percentage of the pupils on the bus are wearing glasses?

   %

   2 marks

4) Look at the diagram on the right.

   What is the area of the rectangle? cm^2

   13 cm

   1 mark

   d

   5 cm

   What is the size of angle d? °

   21°

   1 mark

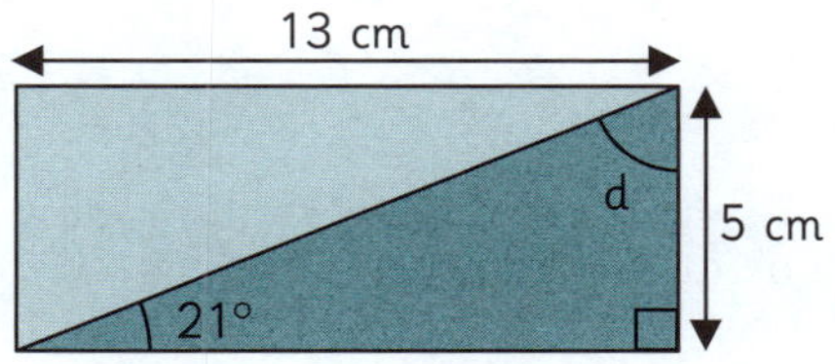

5) Find the next two terms in each of these sequences.

   32   38   44

   1 mark

   7   3   −1

   1 mark

© CGP — not to be photocopied

Section 1 Progress Test

6) Complete the calculations below.

$400 \times 8 =$

____
1 mark

$630 \div 30 =$

____
1 mark

7) Suzie drove to a campsite for a holiday.
The graph shows how far she drove on part of her journey.

How far had she driven
after 1.5 hours? km

____
1 mark

The total distance to the campsite is 300 km.
How much further does Suzie need to drive after 4 hours? km

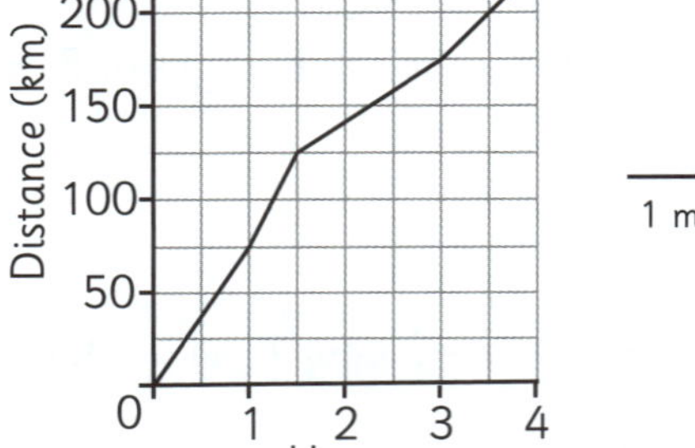

____
1 mark

8) Find the value of the letters in each of the equations below.

$4p = 48$ $p =$

____
1 mark

$q - 8 = 12$ $q =$

____
1 mark

9) Look at the coordinate grid on the right.

What are the new coordinates of point A
after the shape is reflected in the y-axis?

$A =$

____
1 mark

What are the new coordinates of point B
after the shape is translated 4 units
to the right and 2 units up?

$B =$

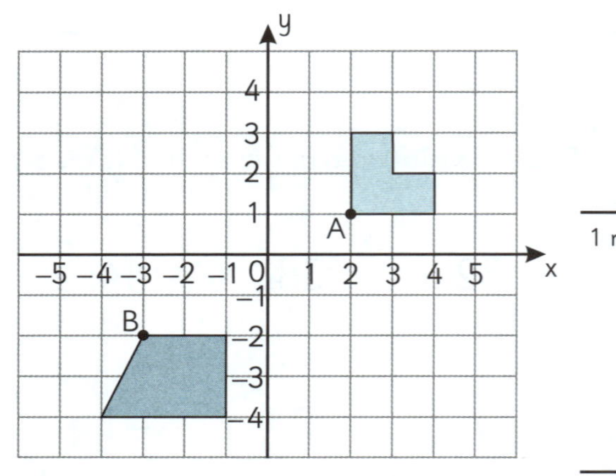

____
1 mark

  © CGP — not to be photocopied

Section 1 Listening Tests

Go to cgpbooks.co.uk/MA-Year6 or scan the QR code on the right to find the audio files for these listening tests. Listen carefully to each question before writing down your answer in the spaces provided for each test.

Each test has ten questions. You will have 5 seconds to answer each of the first five questions, and 10 seconds to answer each of the last five questions.

Section 1
Listening Tests

Listening Test 1

1. ....
2. ....
3. .... %
4. ....

5. ....
6. ....
7. £ ....

8. ....
9. .... cm^2
10. .... mins

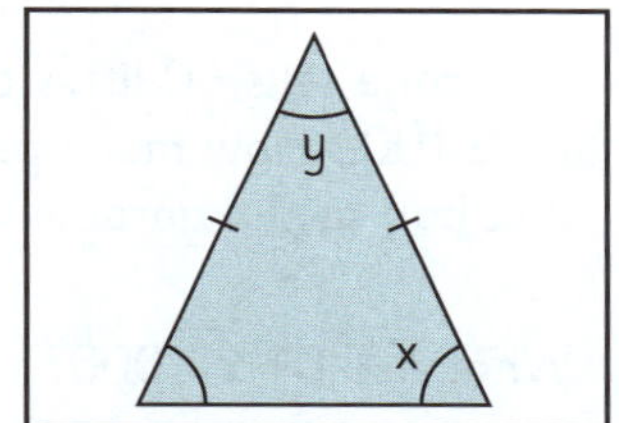

Listening Test 2

1. .... g
2. ....
3. ....
4. ....

5. ....
6. ....
7. ....

8. .... km
9. ....
10. .... °

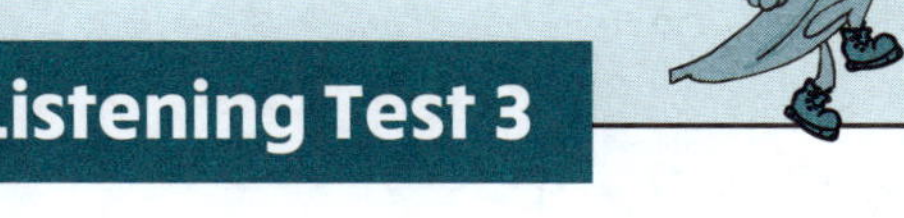

Listening Test 3

1. ....
2. .... %
3. ....
4. ....

5. l
6. £ ....
7. ....

8. .... cm^2
9. ....
10. ....

Section Two

Test 1

Part A

1. What is 3990 + 4006?   ....

2. Convert 1328 m to km.   .... km

3. $\frac{1}{3}$ of $\boxed{?}$ = 33
What is the missing number?   ....

4. Identify the number in the box below that is a multiple of both 8 and 12:

   $\boxed{36 \quad 48 \quad 64}$ ....

5. Sally did 5 science tests and got a mean mark of 14. How many marks did she get in total?   ....

6. What is the missing number that makes 5730 ÷ $\boxed{?}$ = 57.3 correct?   ....

7. Last year, £5 824 225 was donated to a charity. What is the value of the digit in the ten thousands position?   ....

8. Work out 55% of 300.   ....

9. A garage sells 60 litres of petrol for £100. How much petrol could you buy at the garage with £10?   l

10. What is 0.01 × 1000?   ....

11. Look at this formula: p = 45 + 5t. Work out the value of p when t = 5.   ....

12. What is 10 miles in kilometres? Use the conversion 5 miles ≈ 8 km.   .... km

13. Work out $\frac{5}{7} - \frac{3}{14}$, giving your answer in its simplest form.   ....

14. A pencil weighs 0.045 kg. How much does it weigh in grams?   .... g

15. The temperature in Moscow is −5 °C. The temperature in New York is 17 °C. What is the difference in temperature between New York and Moscow?   .... °C

Part B

16. In a cafe, for every 2 cups of coffee that George makes, Harris makes 3. They make 35 cups between them. How many cups does George make?   ....

17. Which is smaller: $\frac{5}{7}$ or $\frac{2}{3}$?   ....

18. A triangle is 4 cm tall and has an area of 16 cm². How long is its base?   .... cm

19. What is the 2nd term in the sequence with first term 28 and rule "add 13"?   ....

20. A rope is $\frac{1}{3}$ m long. It is cut into 5 equal pieces. How long is each piece?   .... m

21. What is the highest common factor of 12 and 16?   ....

22. Work out 4000 × 50.   ....

23. Gareth's suitcase weighs 7.85 kg. He takes out a 430 g pair of jeans. How much does it weigh now?   .... kg

24. What is the size of angle h?   .... ° 

25. A weight is dropped from a 15 m diving board and lands 3 m below the surface of the water. How far did it fall?   .... m

26. What is 52 × 9?   ....

27. Work out 7 + 54 ÷ 9.   ....

28. A carton holds 0.7 litres of juice. How many litres of juice do 3 cartons hold?   l

29. What is 60 hours in days and hours?   .... days .... hours

30. A factory makes 9000 gold baubles and 12 times as many red baubles. How many red baubles do they make?   ....

© CGP — not to be photocopied

Test 2

Warm Up Questions

1) How many minutes are there in one hour?

2) Using your answer to question 1, work out how many minutes there are in 12 hours.

Part A

1. Find the area of a triangle with a height of 7 cm and a base of 8 cm. .... cm²

2. What is 1 902 758 rounded to the nearest 1000? ....

3. A pencil costs 30p. How much will 25 pencils cost? £...................

4. The temperature in a freezer is −17 °C. It increases by 11 °C. What is the temperature in the freezer now? .... °C

5. Work out the size of angle a.

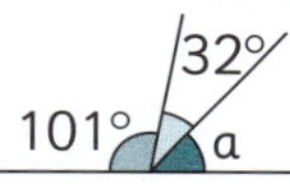

.... °

6. Work out $\frac{2}{15} + \frac{7}{10}$. Give your answer in its simplest form. ....

7. This pie chart shows how 20 people voted in an election. What angle represents one vote on the pie chart?

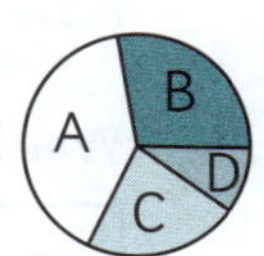

.... °

8. A sequence has first term 10 and rule "add 3". What is the 3rd term? ....

9. A company sells 2 300 000 pens in June, and 3 000 400 pens in July. How many do they sell in total? ....

10. Work out 12 − 24 ÷ 4. ....

11. This formula is used when making soup.

number of leeks = 3 × number of onions

Jem uses 4 onions. How many leeks does she need? ....

12. ? − 22 ÷ 2 = 30 What is the missing number? ....

Part B

13. A drink is made from 68% orange juice. What fraction is not orange juice? Give your answer in its simplest form. ....

14. Which of these fractions is the smallest?

$2\frac{1}{2}$ $\frac{7}{2}$ $\frac{6}{4}$

....

15. Which is greater: 0.65 kg or 640 g? ....

16. Tomasz plays a game with 6 levels. The maximum score on each level is 203. What is the most points Tomasz could score in total on all 6 levels? ....

17. What is the lowest common multiple of 2, 6 and 11? ....

18. Which is larger, A: 90% of 500 or B: 40% of 1000? ....

19. Sofia is reading a series of books that each have 210 pages. She reads 70 pages a day. How many books does she read in 6 days? ....

20. 5 475 240 people live in Tretham. Round this to the nearest ten thousand. ....

21. What is the missing number that makes 18 + 10 × ? = 88 correct? ....

22. Tara and Ewan pay for a video game in the ratio 3 : 4. The game costs £42. How much does Tara pay? £...................

23. What is 0.7 × 6? ....

24. Ben visits a friend who lives 72 km away. How far is this in miles? Use the conversion 5 miles ≈ 8 km. .... miles

© CGP — not to be photocopied

Test 3

Part A

1. Work out the mean of 30, 10 and 80. ....

2. What is the next term in this sequence?
4, −5, −14, −23, $\boxed{?}$ ....

3. What is $\frac{3}{4} \div 7$? ....

4. Work out the lowest common multiple of 6 and 10. ....

5. Find the value of T when x = 5 and y = 6. $\boxed{T = \frac{xy}{2}}$ ....

6. Convert 32 km into miles. Use the conversion 5 miles ≈ 8 km .... miles

7. Which of the numbers below rounds to 5 270 000 to the nearest 10?

$\boxed{\begin{array}{cc} 5\ 259\ 799 & 5\ 269\ 995 \\ & 5\ 269\ 993 \end{array}}$ ....

8. What is the missing number that makes $\boxed{?} + 5 \times 4 = 39$ correct? ....

9. Work out $\frac{3}{5} \times \frac{1}{6}$, giving your answer in its simplest form. ....

10. A point, p, is at (−5, 4). It is translated 6 units right and 8 units down. What are the new coordinates of p? ....

11. What is the area of this triangle?
.... cm²

12. Write down the biggest prime number between 40 and 50. ....

13. Hanan has 593.5 grams of dough. He splits it into 10 equal balls. How much does each ball weigh? .... g

14. What is the missing number?
$3\frac{5}{7}$ weeks = ... days

15. At a shop, 200 of every 1000 bikes sold are BMXs. 8000 bikes are sold. How many are BMXs? ....

Part B

16. Which is smaller,
A: 25% of 200 or B: 20% of 150? ....

17. A rectangle has a perimeter of 14 cm. It is 4 cm wide. How tall is it? .... cm

18. Billy has −£20 in his bank account. He gets a payment of £44. How much money is in his bank account now? £................

19. $\frac{5}{6} + \frac{3}{8} = \frac{?}{24}$
What is the missing number? ....

20. Convert 420 seconds into minutes. .... mins

21. In one week, Yas did 64 410 steps and Dom did 50 300 steps. How many more steps did Yas do than Dom? ....

22. A company made £1 528 600 in a year. How much money did they make to the nearest ten thousand pounds? £................

23. What is 508 × 6? ....

24. Asma and Jim recorded how far they cycled in a day. In total they cycled 9.4 km. Jim cycled 4.3 km. How far did Asma cycle, in metres? .... m

25. Which of these amounts is largest?
$\boxed{28\% \quad \frac{1}{5} \quad 0.25}$ ....

26. What is 1070 − 406? ....

27. Carlos jogs $3\frac{2}{3}$ km.
Felicia jogs $\frac{10}{3}$ km.
Who jogs further? ....

28. What is $\frac{1}{4}$ of 300? ....

29. Diaz ran 50 km in a weekend. The ratio of the distance he ran on Saturday to the distance he ran on Sunday is 7 : 3. How far did he run on Sunday? .... km

30. What is 95 − 12 × 7? ....

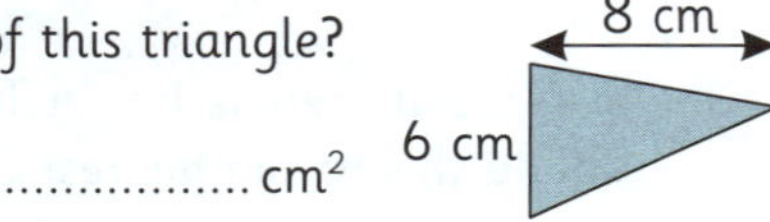

© CGP — not to be photocopied

Test 4

Part A

1. Convert 5870 ml into litres. l

2. A vet sees 5 dogs, 20 cats and 25 fish. What percentage of the pets are dogs? .... %

3. 1 927 884 people visit an art gallery in one year. What is the value of the digit in the hundred thousands position? ....

4. What is the third term in the sequence with the rule 2n + 4? ....

5. Which is smaller: $\frac{27}{12}$ or $2\frac{1}{12}$? ....

6. A shed is built out of oak and pine logs. 5 oak logs are used for every 7 pine logs. 48 logs are used in total. How many oak logs are used? ....

7. $\frac{2}{3} \times \frac{?}{5} = \frac{8}{15}$
What is the missing number? ....

8. What is 37 − 8 × 3? ....

9. Write down one common multiple of 2, 3 and 4 between 30 and 40. ....

10. What is 3 992 417 rounded to the nearest hundred thousand? ....

11. This pie chart shows the colours of shirts in a shop. What fraction of the shirts are pink? ....

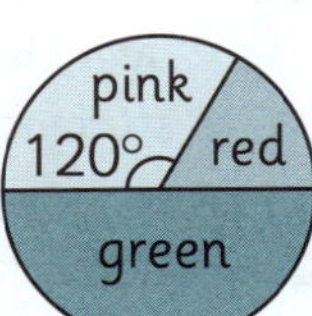

12. A rectangle has an area of 48 cm² and a base of 6 cm. What is its height? .... cm

13. What is $\frac{17}{12} - \frac{1}{4}$ in its simplest form? ....

14. A fun run raises £252 085 for charity. A bake sale raises another £10 700. How much money is raised in total? £ ....

15. Megan buys a bed for £123. She spends £60 fixing it up, then sells it for £200. How much profit does she make? £ ....

Part B

16. Andy's piano lesson lasts 165 minutes. Ruth's lesson lasts 1 hour 20 minutes. How many minutes shorter is Ruth's lesson than Andy's? .... mins

17. What is $\frac{2}{7}$ of 21? ....

18. What is the angle i in this kite? .... °

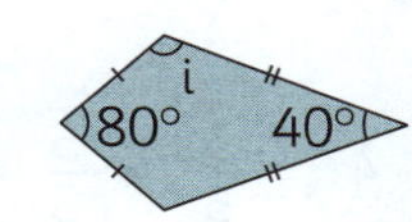

19. A freezer's temperature is −14 °C. Jon's kitchen is 20 °C. How much warmer is Jon's kitchen than the freezer? .... °C

20. What will the value of the digit 5 be after 354.8 is divided by 100? ....

21. What is 8.1 × 8? ....

22. How far is 64 km in miles? Use the conversion 5 miles ≈ 8 km. .... miles

23. △ = 50 × ◯ + 12. If ◯ = 3, what is the value of △? ....

24. A parallelogram has a base of 6 cm and a height of 3 cm. What is its area? .... cm²

25. What is 96 000 ÷ 80? ....

26. Sarah has 1 kg of flour. She uses $\frac{3}{5}$ of the flour to make some bread. How much flour does she have left? .... kg

27. What is the highest common factor of 36 and 48? ....

28. What is the missing number that makes ? + 84 ÷ 7 = 17 correct? ....

29. 3 in every 25 people who play a game win a prize. 100 people play the game. How many win a prize? ....

30. What is 525.8 cm in metres? .... m

© CGP — not to be photocopied

Section Two

Test 5

Part A

1. What is $\frac{5}{9} \div 5$ in its simplest form? ....

2. What is 8 764 072 rounded to the nearest 100 000? ....

3. Nabil's fish tank holds 7.8 litres of water. How many ml of water does it hold? .... ml

4. $\frac{\boxed{?}}{5} \times \frac{5}{8} = \frac{1}{4}$
   What is the missing number? ....

5. A pack of biscuits costs £1.60. What is the cost of 8 packs of biscuits? £ ....

6. What is $\frac{9}{20}$ as a percentage? .... %

7. A parallelogram has a height of 5 cm and base of 13 cm. What is its area? .... cm^2

8. What is $5400 \div 60$? ....

9. Simone dives down to 23 m below sea level. Bailey is watching from a cliff 46 m above sea level. How far is Bailey above Simone, in metres?

.... m

10. Work out $6 \times 35 \div 7$. ....

11. Ellie rounds the number 5 287 341 to get 5 290 000. Has she rounded to the nearest 100, 1000 or 10 000? ....

12. Use the graph to convert £14 to Swiss francs.

.... Fr.

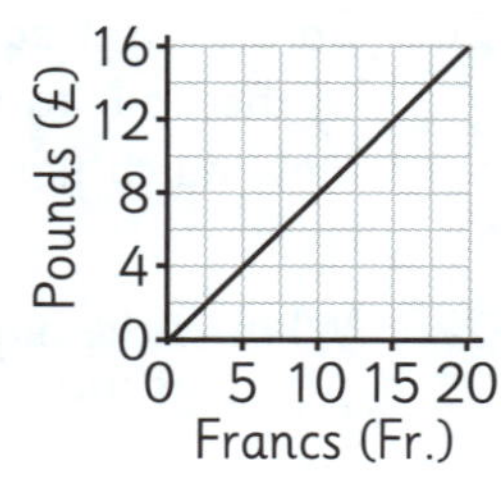

13. What is the fourth term of the sequence with the rule $5n - 2$? ....

14. There is one screw for every five nails in a table. There are 60 screws and nails in total. How many screws are there? ....

15. Jess lives 4.8 km away from the park. How far is this in metres? .... m

Part B

16. Which distance is further, A: 1.383 cm or B: 13.48 mm? ....

17. What is 1.2×9? ....

18. Shape F is reflected in the y-axis. What are the new coordinates of point P?

....

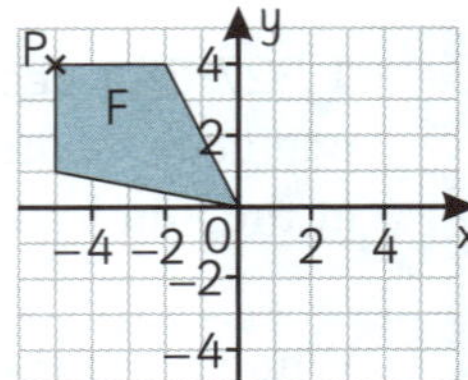

19. Identify the prime number below.

| 21 | 35 | 31 | 18 |

....

20. Using the formula $A = wh$, work out the value of A when $w = 7$ and $h = 4$. ....

21. What is 5.859 litres in ml? .... ml

22. In a long jump competition, Olivia jumps $2\frac{2}{5}$ m and Gavin jumps 2.3 metres. Who jumps further? ....

23. On a farm there are 2 cows for every 5 chickens. There are 12 cows in total. How many chickens are there? ....

24. What is the missing number that makes $71\ 200 \div \boxed{?} = 7.12$ correct? ....

25. In a survey of 252 students, 160 were over the age of 21. How many of the students were aged 21 or under? ....

26. Convert 1000 miles to kilometres. Use the conversion 5 miles ≈ 8 km. .... km

27. Which of these numbers is the smallest?

$\frac{11}{9} \qquad 1\frac{2}{3} \qquad 1\frac{5}{9}$

....

28. Work out $\frac{1}{6} + \frac{7}{30}$, giving your answer in its simplest form. ....

29. What is $205\ 420 - 104\ 000$? ....

30. How many common factors do 24 and 36 have? ....

© CGP — not to be photocopied

Test 6

Warm Up Questions

1) Look at the grid on the right. What percentage of it is shaded?

2) What proportion of the grid on the right is not shaded?
   Give your answer as a fraction in its simplest form.

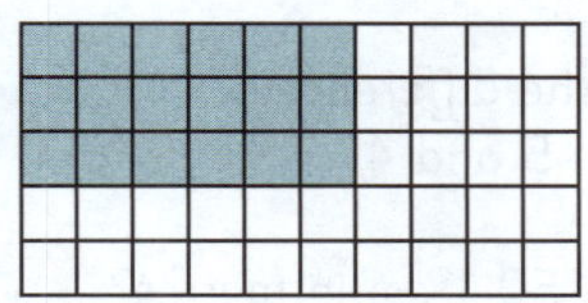

Part A

1. What is 77 000 ÷ 7? ....

2. Write down the next number in this sequence: 1.4, 1.9, 2.4, ? ....

3. A lift is on floor −6. It travels up 25 floors. What floor is it on now? ....

4. The cost of a parking ticket is:

   cost in £ = 2 × hours parked + 1.5

   How much does a 3-hour ticket cost? £ ....

5. There are 20 pupils in a class. 15 of them have brown hair. What percentage of the pupils have brown hair? .... %

6. A recipe uses 3 eggs for every 200 g of flour. Mika uses 9 eggs. How much flour does he need? .... g

7. Lea has driven 72 000 miles in 9 years. She drives the same distance every year. How far does she drive each year? .... miles

8. Work out $\frac{4}{7} \times \frac{1}{8}$, giving your answer in its simplest form. ....

9. Liam babysits two 6-year-olds and three 11-year-olds. What is the mean age of all the children he babysits? ....

10. Find a prime number that is also a common factor of 28 and 63. ....

11. Which of these numbers rounds to 952 000 to the nearest 100?

    952 104   951 964   951 896 ....

12. Nawra runs 16 km for charity. How many miles does she run? Use the conversion 5 miles ≈ 8 km. .... miles

Part B

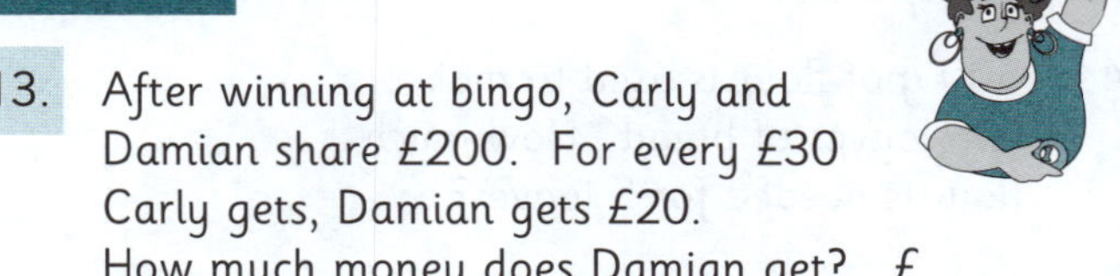

13. After winning at bingo, Carly and Damian share £200. For every £30 Carly gets, Damian gets £20. How much money does Damian get? £ ....

14. $\frac{9}{4} - \frac{5}{6} = \frac{?}{12}$
    What is the missing number? ....

15. It costs £0.96 to make one bracelet. How much would it cost to make 100 bracelets? £ ....

16. Which is smaller: 0.08 litres or 800 ml? ....

17. What is the missing fraction? Give your answer in its simplest form.
    $\frac{?}{?} \div 2 = \frac{7}{16}$ ....

18. What is 23 + 6 × 11? ....

19. Which is smaller: $\frac{7}{20}$ or 0.4? ....

20. What is the missing number that makes $\boxed{?} - 6 \times 2 = 5$ correct? ....

21. Find the biggest fraction in the list below.

    $\frac{13}{3}$ $\frac{10}{6}$ $\frac{7}{3}$ ....

22. What is the size of angle d?  ....°

23. $\frac{1}{6}$ of the stamps in Rico's collection are red. If Rico has 20 red stamps, how many stamps must he have in total? ....

24. What is the area of this parallelogram? 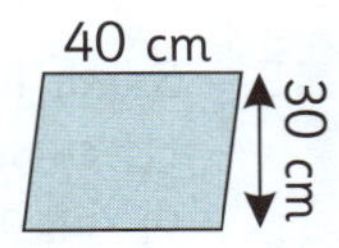
    .... cm²

© CGP — not to be photocopied

Test 7

Part A

1. What is the difference between −5 and 4? ....

2. What is 150.1 cm in metres? .... m

3. What is the value of the even digit in the number 7 731 895? ....

4. 500 g of flour is used to make two loaves of bread. How much flour is needed for 5 loaves? .... g

5. Work out the size of angle a. ....°

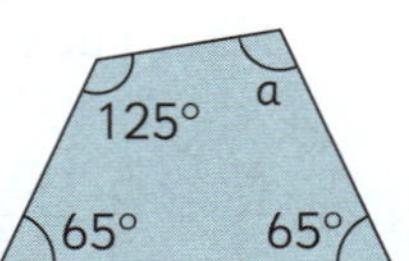

6. Which is bigger: $\frac{5}{4}$ or $\frac{9}{8}$? ....

7. A rectangular playing field is 5.5 m wide and 12 m long. What is the area of the field? .... m²

8. Work out 562 ÷ 100. ....

9. A cafe uses 95 onions and 110 peppers a day. How many onions and peppers do they use in total each week? ....

10. Add ten to fifteen, then divide seventy-five by the result. ....

11. A bottle holds $\frac{3}{4}$ litres of juice. How much juice is in $\frac{1}{2}$ a bottle? l

12. The ratio of rollerbladers to skateboarders in a skate park is 3:5. There are 40 rollerbladers and skateboarders in total. How many rollerbladers are there?

....

13. What is 56 km in miles? Use the conversion 5 miles ≈ 8 km. .... miles

14. $\frac{1}{2}$ of $\boxed{?}$ = 15 What is the missing number? ....

15. Samir has a 1.85 m piece of ribbon. He cuts 125 cm off. How many cm of ribbon does he have left? .... cm

Part B

16. What is the third term of the sequence with the rule 4n + 1? ....

17. Paula runs $\frac{3}{4}$ km and Dara runs $\frac{5}{6}$ km. How much further did Dara run, as a fraction in its simplest form? .... km

18. How many minutes are in 8 hours? .... mins

19. Look at the formula p = 3q + 4. What is p when q = 2? ....

20. What is 8400 ÷ 12? ....

21. A phone is discounted by 45% in a sale. It originally cost £220. How much cheaper is it in the sale? £.................

22. Write down the common factor of 15 and 27 that is greater than 1. ....

23. Which number in the box below rounds to 6 570 000 to the nearest ten thousand?

6 579 418	6 575 034
6 568 932	6 564 989

....

24. What is $\frac{120}{500}$ as a decimal? ....

25. The area of this triangle is 15 mm². What is length b? .... mm

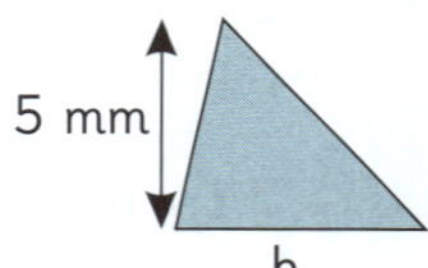

26. $\boxed{?}$ − (2 × 8) = 4 What is the missing number? ....

27. A sketch pad costs £8.50. How much would 8 sketch pads cost? £.................

28. Luis makes the same amount of jam each month. In a year, he makes 7200 kg. How many kg of jam does he make each month? .... kg

29. Find the mean of 8, 12 and 7. ....

30. A lollipop costs 5p. How much would 104 lollipops cost in pence? ....p

© CGP — not to be photocopied

Test 8

Part A

1. Round 2 386 455 to the nearest thousand. ....

2. Convert 3.9 cm to mm. .... mm

3. What is 80 × 3000? ....

4. Find the area of this parallelogram.

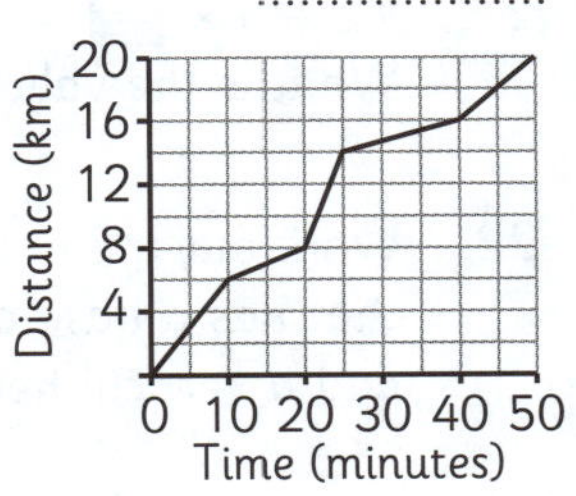

.... cm²

5. Asha does a ballet class for 55 minutes and a tap class for 1 hour 15 minutes. How long is she in classes for in total, in hours and minutes? .... hours .... mins

6. Each month, 7500 people visit a castle. 3500 visitors are 18 or under. How many over 18s visit the castle in a year? ....

7. What is the next term in the sequence 17, 25, 33, 41, ...? ....

8. The temperature in Toronto is −2 °C. In Athens, it is 25 °C warmer. What temperature is it in Athens? .... °C

9. Find the missing number:
4 607 000 − $\boxed{?}$ = 807 000 ....

10. A pot of orange paint is made from 1600 ml of yellow paint and 900 ml of red paint. How much orange paint is in 3 pots? .... ml

11. $2p + 7 = 11$
What is the value of p? ....

12. What is 15% of 60? ....

13. This graph shows how far Suzi cycled during a race. How far had she cycled after 25 minutes?

.... km

14. Which is smaller: $\frac{16}{25}$ or 65%? ....

15. The area of a rectangle is 12 cm². It is 2 cm wide. How long is it? .... cm

© CGP — not to be photocopied

Part B

16. An ice cream van sells 2 tubs for every 5 cones they sell. They sell 25 cones. How many tubs do they sell?

....

17. Work out 2.17 × 10. ....

18. A relay race is $\frac{2}{5}$ km long. It is split into 4 equal parts. How many km is each part, as a fraction in its simplest form? .... km

19. Which of the numbers between 50 and 55 is a prime number? ....

20. Which is further: 2 miles or 4 km? Use the conversion 5 miles ≈ 8 km. ....

21. What is $\frac{13}{20} - \frac{2}{5}$ in its simplest form? ....

22. What is the size of angle h?

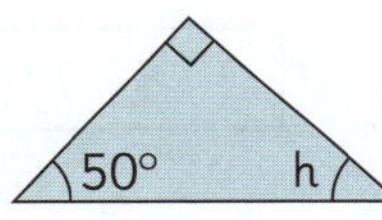

.... °

23. A bag of dog food weighs 3.2 kg. How much would 9 bags weigh? .... kg

24. Which fraction below would be in the middle if they were put in ascending order?

$$\frac{24}{10} \qquad \frac{11}{5} \qquad 1\frac{3}{5}$$

....

25. What is 2.005 kg in grams? .... g

26. Jack and Finley share £60 in the ratio 1 : 4. How much does Jack get? £ ....

27. What is the smallest number that is a common multiple of 3 and 8? ....

28. Work out $\frac{3}{8}$ of 40. ....

29. Evanna decorates 2400 biscuits with 4 sweets each. How many sweets will she need to decorate them all? ....

30. 520 people go on a coach trip. Each coach seats 50 people. How many coaches are needed? ....

Test 9

Warm Up Questions

Choose an operation from the box on the right to make each of these calculations correct.

× 10	÷ 10
× 100	÷ 100
× 1000	÷ 1000

1) 4.37 ☐ = 4370

2) 983 ☐ = 9.83

Part A

1. Convert 18 ml to litres. l

2. What is the value of the 6 after 10 576 is divided by 1000? ....

3. Write $\frac{9}{20}$ as a decimal. ....

4. The anchor of a boat is 10 m under water. A flag on the boat's mast is 8 m above the water. What is the vertical distance between the anchor and the flag? .... m

5. Which number in the box is not prime?

2	5	7	15	19

....

6. One serving of cereal weighs 25 g. Freddie has 0.525 kg of cereal. How many servings does he have? ....

7. What is 150 × 800? ....

8. 5 people share £3200 equally. How much does each person get? £ ....

9. Gina delivers 220 parcels every day. How many does she deliver in 7 days? ....

10. Find the area of this triangle.

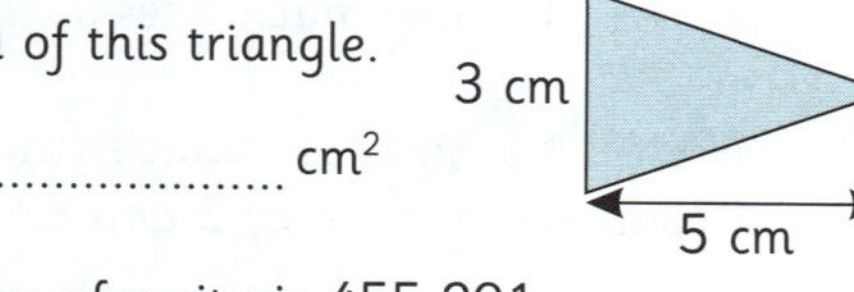

.... cm^2

11. The population of a city is 455 201. What is the population of the city to the nearest ten thousand? ....

12. What is $\frac{13}{9} - \frac{11}{18}$ in its simplest form? ....

13. Kriti ran 24 km. Use the conversion 5 miles ≈ 8 km to work out how far she ran in miles. .... miles

Part B

14. A lap of a race track is 2.8 km. How many kilometres is 5 laps? .... km

15. What will the coordinates of point P be after it has been reflected in the x-axis?

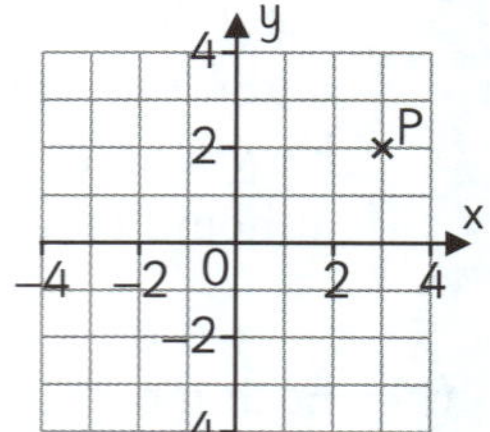

....

16. Which of these fractions is the biggest?

$\frac{7}{4}$	$\frac{5}{2}$	$\frac{15}{8}$

....

17. A sequence begins 7, 10, 13, 16, ... What is the sixth term? ....

18. 120 people in a survey were asked their favourite sport. 35% said football. How many people said football? ....

19. Work out 6 × (88 ÷ 11). ....

20. Romesh has 110 DVDs. $\frac{2}{11}$ of them are comedy DVDs. How many comedy DVDs does he have? ....

21. 12 + 5 × ☐ = 17 What is the value of ☐? ....

22. Work out the area of a parallelogram that has a base of length 7 cm and a vertical height of 9 cm. .... cm^2

23. What is the mean of 7, 11, 6 and 8? ....

24. Polly has 3 red pens for every 4 blue pens. She has 35 red and blue pens in total. How many red pens does she have? ....

© CGP — not to be photocopied

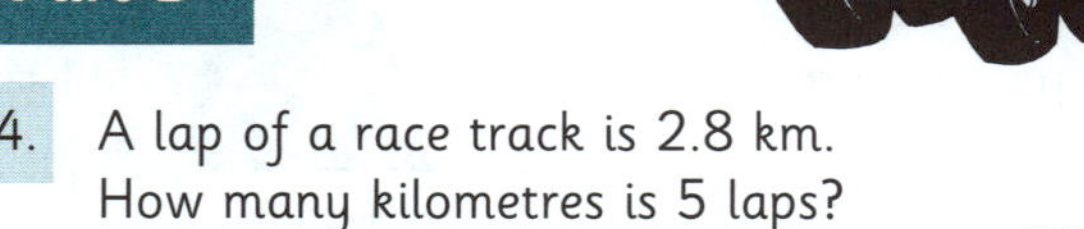

Test 10

Part A

1. Work out 0.27 × 100. ....

2. What is the difference between −17 and −9? ....

3. Which is a smaller amount: 90 g or 0.009 kg? ....

4. 4 050 938 rounds to 4 050 000. Has it been rounded to the nearest 100, 1000 or 10 000? ....

5. Write the number that is 100 times smaller than 2896. ....

6. Small boxes hold 12 plants and large boxes hold 35 plants. How many plants can 5 small boxes and 2 large boxes hold? ....

7. What is 0.8 × 7? ....

8. What is the fifth term of the sequence with the rule 5n − 3? ....

9. Put these amounts in order, starting with the largest.

$$0.8 \qquad \frac{17}{20} \qquad 83\%$$

....

10. One cake weighs 0.87 kg and another cake weighs $\frac{19}{20}$ kg. What is their total weight in kg as a decimal? .... kg

11. Fill in the missing number:
$3 \times (56 \div \boxed{?}) = 24$ ....

12. What is the size of angle c? .... °

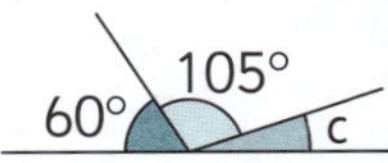

13. There are 2600 beads in a jar. Huw takes 200 for himself, then shares the rest between four friends. How many does each friend get? ....

14. What is $\frac{1}{4} \times \frac{4}{5}$ in its simplest form? ....

15. Matt walked 3.8 km. Jacinda walked 255 m further than Matt. How many metres did Jacinda walk? .... m

Part B

16. A bag contains 90 sweets in three different flavours, shown on this pie chart. How many lemon sweets are there? ....

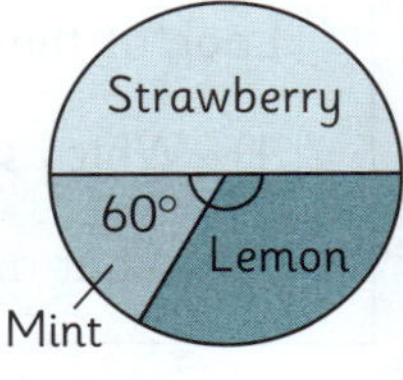

17. What is 210 500 + 600 000? ....

18. 3 in every 8 pupils in Ugne's class are blonde. There are 24 pupils in her class. How many are blonde? ....

19. How many common factors do 15 and 36 have? ....

20. Holly spent $\frac{1}{3}$ of her pocket money on a poster and $\frac{2}{5}$ on a book. What fraction did she spend in total? ....

21. $3x − 1 = 11$
What is the value of x? ....

22. A triangle has a vertical height of 11 cm and a base of 6 cm. What is its area? .... cm^2

23. What is 25 miles in kilometres? Use the conversion 5 miles ≈ 8 km. .... km

24. What is 5% of 200? ....

25. In a pack of marbles, $\frac{1}{3}$ are green. There are 12 green marbles. How many are in the pack? ....

26. What is 8 × (7 − 3)? ....

27. A bowl can hold 4.5 litres of batter. There is 1250 ml of batter in it. How much more could it hold in ml? .... ml

28. This parallelogram has an area of 24 m^2. What is its vertical height? .... m

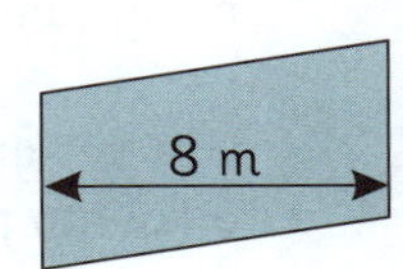

29. What is 5 948 254 rounded to the nearest hundred thousand? ....

30. 6 T-shirts cost £54 in total. How much would 3 T-shirts cost? £ ....

© CGP — not to be photocopied

Section Two

Test 11

Warm Up Questions

Look at the four sequences in the box on the right.

1) Which sequence can be generated using the rule 3n + 1?

2) What are the next two terms of sequence D?

A: 3, 6, 9, 12, ...
B: 4, 5, 6, 7, ...
C: 4, 7, 10, 13, ...
D: 2, 5, 8, 11, ...

Part A

1. Round 7 503 278 to the nearest million. ....

2. How many common factors of 30 and 40 are also prime numbers? ....

3. A gallery has 1 482 395 visitors in one year. Which digit is in the hundred thousands position? ....

4. Look at the formula $A = \dfrac{B}{4} + 5$. What is A when B = 12? ....

5. What is 1520 m + 1.07 km in kilometres? .... km

6. A bag contains 40 sponge balls. 1 in every 5 is green. How many balls in the bag are green? ....

7. What is the area of this parallelogram? .... m²

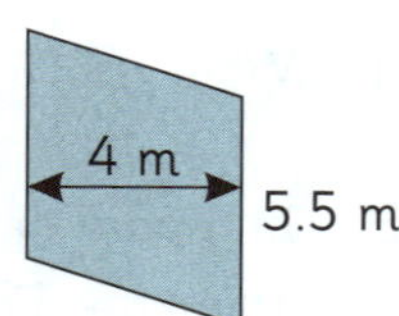

8. Use the conversion 5 miles ≈ 8 km to work out 72 km in miles. .... miles

9. What is 8.4 × 3? ....

10. An aquarium has 279 clownfish. Each tank holds 9 clownfish. How many tanks of clownfish are there? ....

11. Use this graph to convert 6 kg into pounds (lb). .... lb

12. Find the lowest common multiple of 4 and 9. ....

Part B

13. $\dfrac{3}{10}$ of Meera's stamps are red, $\dfrac{1}{4}$ are blue and the rest are green. What fraction of her stamps are green? ....

14. Work out the size of angle b. .... °

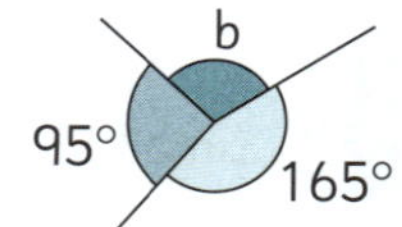

15. What is the difference between the highest and lowest numbers in the box below? ....

−6	2	13	−4

16. What is the next term in the sequence 81, 75, 69, 63, ...? ....

17. $\dfrac{1}{3}$ of tickets sold at a raffle were pink. 450 tickets were sold. How many of them were pink? ....

18. What is 30% of 75? ....

19. A library has 16 800 fiction books. One quarter of them are on loan. How many fiction books are left in the library? ....

20. Work out 3 700 400 − 2 800 000. ....

21. Amy shares $\dfrac{4}{5}$ kg of carrots equally between three rabbits. How much does each rabbit get as a fraction? .... kg

22. The base of a triangle is 14 cm long and its vertical height is 8 cm. What is the area of the triangle? .... cm²

23. Which is bigger: $1\dfrac{1}{5}$ or $\dfrac{9}{8}$? ....

24. What is 60 ÷ (42 ÷ 7)? ....

© CGP — not to be photocopied

Test 12

Part A

1. Work out 894 ÷ 1000. ....

2. How many seconds are in 2 minutes 15 seconds? .... s

3. Find the missing number:
170 300 + ☐ ? = 480 300 ....

4. Ben buys 20% of a 2 kg block of cheese. How much does he buy in grams? .... g

5. The cost C, in £, of going on n rides at a funfair is C = 1 + 2n. How much does it cost to go on 5 rides? £....................

6. Find the highest common factor of 22 and 88. ....

7. Which number in the box below can't have been rounded to the nearest thousand?

2 366 000	4 810 000
5 263 400	8 716 000

....

8. What is 7300 ml – 2.5 litres in ml? .... ml

9. What number between 20 and 40 is a common multiple of 9 and 6? ....

10. A factory prints 4000 books per hour. How many could it print in 60 hours? ....

11. What is the area of this rectangle? .... cm²

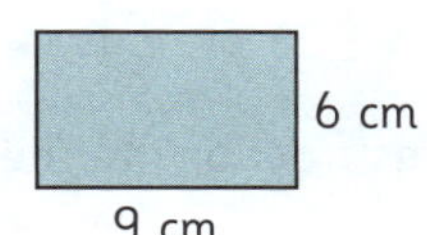

12. Soraya makes 5500 ml of lemonade, and uses it to fill 250 ml bottles. How many bottles does she fill? ....

13. A train ticket costs £9.20. How much do 3 tickets cost? £....................

14. Kai and Binh share a bag of sweets in the ratio 2 : 3. Binh gets 18 sweets. How many sweets does Kai get? ....

15. What is $\frac{5}{6} \div 10$ in its simplest form? ....

16. There are 59 976 fans at a football match. Round this number to the nearest hundred. ....

Part B

17. A lorry travelled 500 miles. How far is this in km? Use the conversion 5 miles ≈ 8 km. .... km

18. What is 12 × (66 ÷ 6)? ....

19. This pie chart shows the types of houses on a street. What fraction of houses on the street are detached? ....

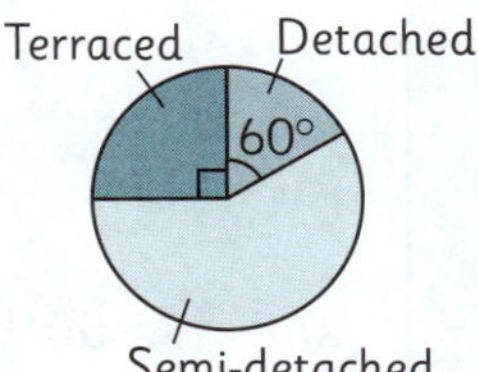

20. 1 in every 5 flowers in a vase are daisies. There are 20 flowers in the vase. How many are daisies? ....

21. Which of these fractions is the smallest?

$$\frac{4}{3} \quad \frac{7}{6} \quad \frac{3}{2}$$

....

22. A box of 20 identical toys weighs 3250 g. The box alone weighs 250 g. How much does one toy weigh? .... g

23. What is 38% as a fraction in its simplest form? ....

24. Yusuf parks his car on level –3, and his flat is on level 14. How many levels does he go up to get from his car to his flat? ....

25. What is $\frac{1}{9}$ of 180? ....

26. A statue sells for £25 000. £7000 of this is donated to charity, and the rest is shared equally between 10 museums. How much does each museum get? £....................

27. What is $\frac{1}{7} + \frac{3}{14}$? ....

28. This triangle is isosceles. What is the size of angle q? .... °

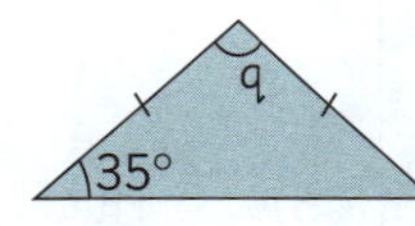

29. The vertical height of a parallelogram is 8 cm and its base length is 11 cm. What is its area? .... cm²

30. Find the missing term in this sequence:
15, ☐ ? , 45, 60, ...

© CGP — not to be photocopied

Section 2 Progress Test

1) An archaeologist finds a vase buried 25 m below sea level and a helmet 12 m below sea level.

What is the vertical distance between the vase and the helmet?

m

1 mark

2) At the beginning of the day, a bookshop has 3397 books. They sell 55 books in the shop and 3 times as many books online, which they post out that day.

How many books do they sell online?

1 mark

How many books do they have left in the shop at the end of the day?

1 mark

3) Look at this formula: $d = m + 3v$.

Work out the value of d when $m = 4$ and $v = 3$.

1 mark

4) Complete these calculations, giving your answers as fractions in their simplest form.

$$\frac{3}{10} \times \frac{2}{6} = \boxed{} \qquad \frac{4}{5} \div 2 = \boxed{}$$

2 marks

5) There are 3 red cars for every 7 silver cars in a car park. Jin counts that there are 84 silver cars.

How many red cars are there?

1 mark

© CGP — not to be photocopied

Section 2 Progress Test

6) What is the mean amount of liquid in the containers below?

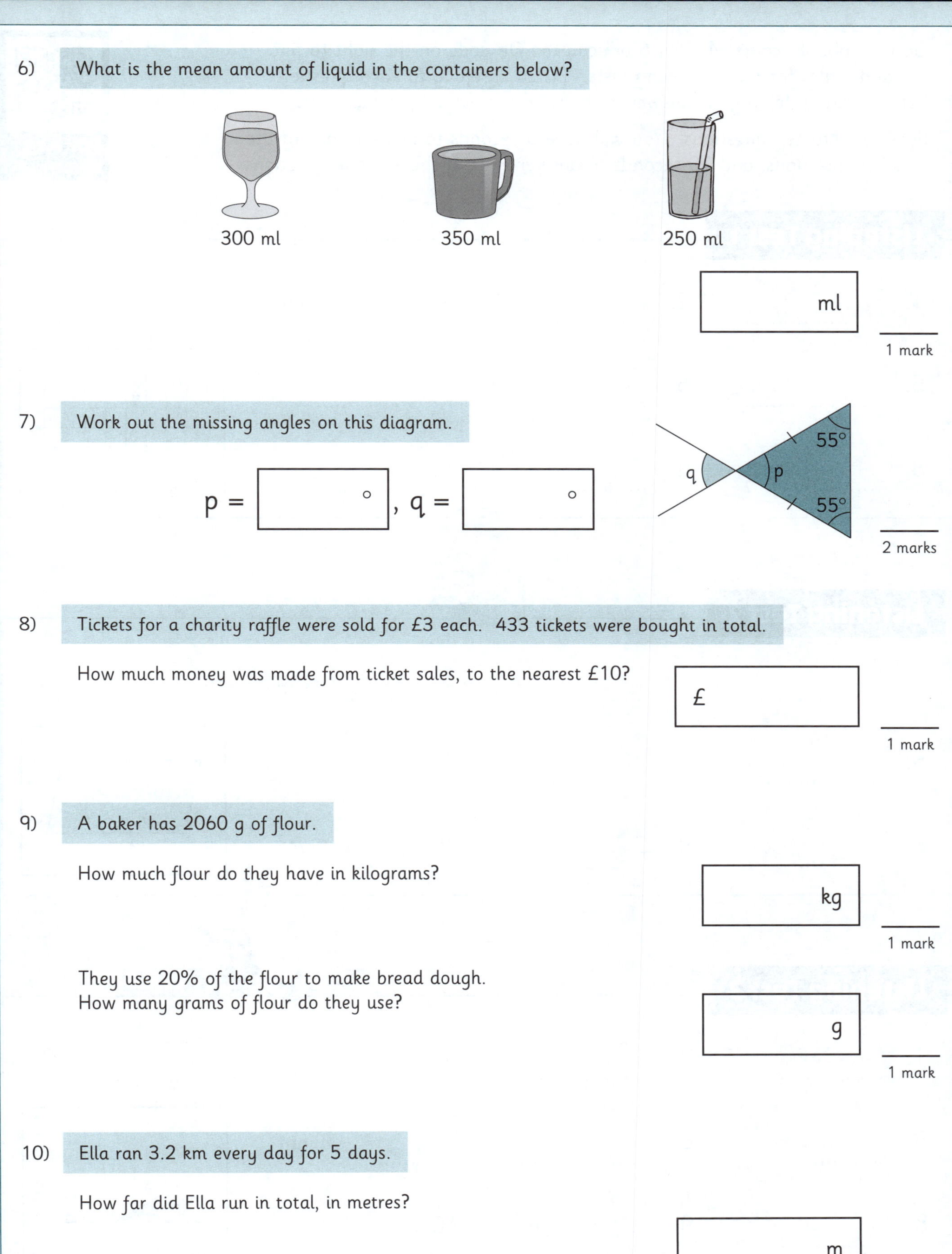

300 ml   350 ml   250 ml

ml

1 mark

7) Work out the missing angles on this diagram.

p = ☐ °, q = ☐ °

2 marks

8) Tickets for a charity raffle were sold for £3 each. 433 tickets were bought in total.

How much money was made from ticket sales, to the nearest £10?

£

1 mark

9) A baker has 2060 g of flour.

How much flour do they have in kilograms?

kg

1 mark

They use 20% of the flour to make bread dough.
How many grams of flour do they use?

g

1 mark

10) Ella ran 3.2 km every day for 5 days.

How far did Ella run in total, in metres?

m

1 mark

Section 2 Listening Tests

Go to cgpbooks.co.uk/MA-Year6 or scan the QR code on the right to find the audio files for these listening tests. Listen carefully to each question before writing down your answer in the spaces provided for each test.

Each test has ten questions. You will have 5 seconds to answer each of the first five questions, and 10 seconds to answer each of the last five questions.

Listening Test 1

1. ....

2. ....

3. .... cm

4. ....

5. ....

6. ....

7. ....

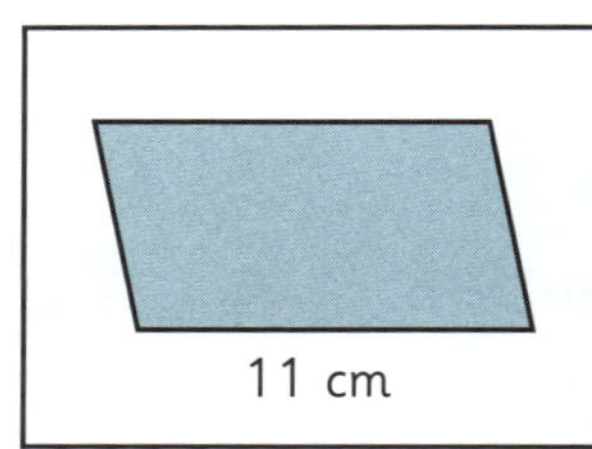

8. .... hours

9. ....

10. ....

Listening Test 2

1. ....

2. ....

3. .... kg

4. ....

5. ....

6. ....

7. ....

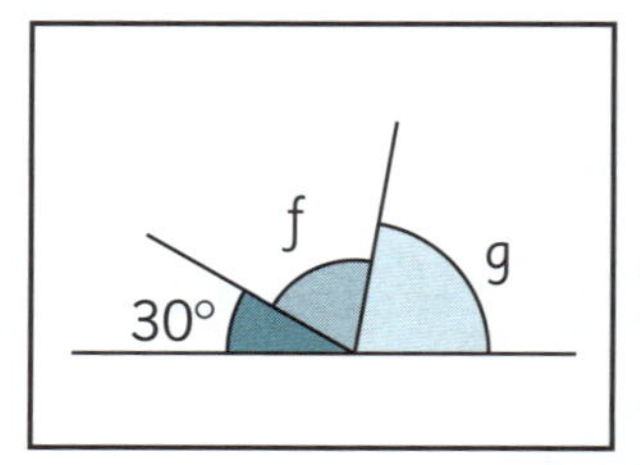

8. .... km

9. £ ....

10. .... cm²

Listening Test 3

1. ....

2. ....

3. ....

4. .... %

5. ....

6. ....

7. .... km

8. .... °

9. .... cm²

10. ....

© CGP — not to be photocopied

Test 1

Part A

1. Convert 900 mm to m. .... m

2. Work out 63 000 ÷ 9. ....

3. How many sixteenths are in $\frac{3}{4}$? ....

4. Harry swims 5.6 km. Mehran swims 250 m further than Harry. How far does Mehran swim in metres? .... m

5. Use the graph below to convert 80 kilometres into miles.

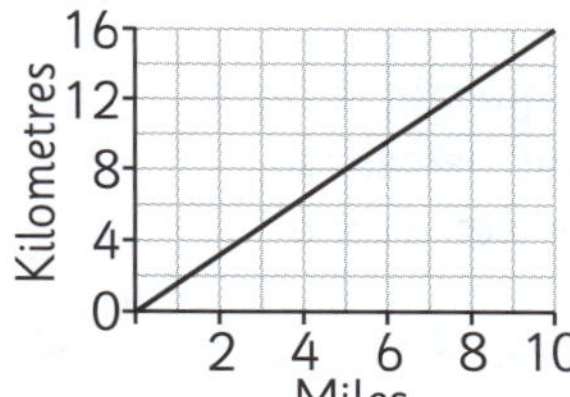

.... miles

6. Hot chocolate is made with 40 g chocolate and 600 ml milk. How much milk is needed to make hot chocolate with 10 g chocolate? .... ml

7. 28 500 + ⬜ = 73 500
   What is the missing number? ....

8. What is 11% of 150? ....

9. Jaime has 5 pieces of ribbon that are each 0.63 m long. How many metres of ribbon does he have in total? .... m

10. What is 38 000 − 17 320 rounded to the nearest hundred? ....

11. p = 60 − 5q
    What is the value of q if p = 45? ....

12. What is $\frac{2}{5}$ of 65? ....

13. Find the area of this parallelogram.

.... cm²

14. What is $\frac{1}{3} + \frac{2}{5}$? ....

15. Stickers cost 20p each. Halima buys 17 stickers and Steve buys 11. How much do they spend in total? £ ....

Part B

16. 80 ÷ 4 + ⭐ = 22
    What is the value of ⭐? ....

17. A cuboid is 8 m long, 5 m wide and 1 m tall. What is the volume of the cuboid? .... m³

18. Naya has £370. She spends £120, then gets £47 for her birthday. How much does she have now? £ ....

19. Convert 75 hours into days and hours.
    .... days .... hours

20. What is $1\frac{5}{6} - \frac{5}{12}$ as an improper fraction? ....

21. What is the size of angle p?

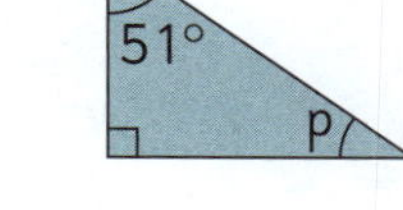

.... °

22. The mean of four numbers is 6. Three of the numbers are 5, 9 and 7. What is the fourth number? ....

23. One day, it is −6 °C in Helsinki and 16 °C in Algiers. How much warmer is it in Algiers? .... °C

24. Write $3\frac{19}{20}$ as a decimal. ....

25. Calculate 9040 × 500. ....

26. A taxi driver uses this formula to work out the cost of a journey.

    cost = (£1.50 × no. of miles) + £3

    What is the cost of a 6-mile journey? £ ....

27. Three angles meet at a point. Two of the angles are 70° and 145°. What is the size of the third angle? .... °

28. Eight cupcakes cost £12. How much would three cupcakes cost? £ ....

29. What is (29 − 12 + 8) ÷ 5? ....

30. The perimeter of a rectangle is 30 cm. The length of its shorter sides is 5 cm. What is the length of its longer sides? .... cm

© CGP — not to be photocopied

Test 2

Part A

1. What is 794 130 ÷ 1000? ....

2. Which is the greater distance:
    $1\frac{2}{3}$ km or $\frac{16}{9}$ km? .... km

3. Clara gives doughnuts to 90 people.
    2 in every 9 of them don't like doughnuts.
    How many of them do like doughnuts? ....

4. 475 000 − $\boxed{?}$ = 195 000
    What is the missing number? ....

5. Trevor eats $\frac{1}{4}$ of a bag of sweets, then
    Anna eats another $\frac{1}{3}$ of the bag. What
    fraction have they eaten in total? ....

6. What is the size of angle a? ....°

7. 6x − 9 = 9
    What is the value of x? ....

8. Jacob buys 10.8 kg of carrots. He uses
    700 g of them to make soup. How many
    kg of carrots does he have left? .... kg

9. What is 5 × 4 − 2? ....

10. Latika was sponsored £S to run d km
    using the formula S = 10 + 3d.
    She raised £25. How far did she run? .... km

11. Find the area of a triangle with a
    height of 6 cm and a base of 10 cm. .... cm²

12. Ibi bought 12 plane tickets, each for the
    same price. They cost £10 800 in total.
    How much did one ticket cost? £ ....

13. Work out $2\frac{5}{6} - 1\frac{1}{3}$. Give your answer
    as a mixed number in its simplest form. ....

14. A rectangle is enlarged by a scale factor
    of 6. After it is enlarged, the length of
    its base is 12 cm. What was the length
    of its base before it was enlarged? .... cm

15. A TV normally costs £290,
    but it is currently 25% off.
    How much cheaper is it currently? £ ....

Part B

16. Imogen draws a pie chart of the
    eye colours of the 30 pupils in her class.
    The 'blue' sector is 120°. How many
    pupils in her class have blue eyes? ....

17. How many common factors
    do 32 and 48 have? ....

18. A cuboid is 12 cm long, 3 cm wide
    and 2 cm tall. What is the volume
    of the cuboid? .... cm³

19. What is 4 × 6.3? ....

20. Ayo got 41 out of 50 questions right
    in a spelling test. What percentage
    of the questions did he get wrong? ....

21. Camilla drove 200 miles. Approximately
    how far did Camilla drive in km?
    Use the conversion 5 miles ≈ 8 km. .... km

22. Find the mean of 11, 23, 19 and 7. ....

23. What is the perimeter of this shape?

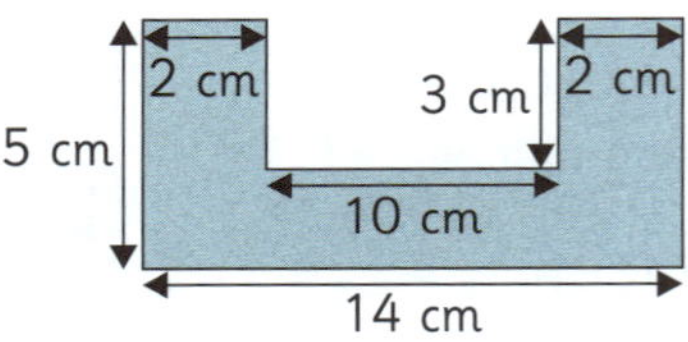

.... cm

24. Work out $\frac{7}{9} - \frac{1}{4}$. ....

25. A bakery sells 9 000 000 loaves
    of bread, to the nearest million.
    What is the smallest number
    of loaves they could have sold?

    ....

26. What is 14 × 40? ....

27. Two of the angles in a triangle
    are 30° and 65°. What is the
    size of the third angle? ....°

28. 156 000 children and 114 000 adults
    visited a theme park one year.
    How many people visited in total? ....

29. What is the fourth term in the
    sequence with the rule 8 + 7n? ....

30. What is $1\frac{3}{4}$ hours in minutes? .... mins

© CGP — not to be photocopied

Test 3

Warm Up Questions

1) What number would you divide by to work out 10% of a number? What about 1% of a number?

2) By first finding 10% of 80 and 1% of 80, work out 31% of 80.

Part A

1. Convert 0.079 km to metres. .... m

2. What is two hundred and forty-six divided by three? ....

3. Round 8.67 to the nearest tenth. ....

4. This shape is made of identical cubes. Each cube has a volume of 4 cm³.

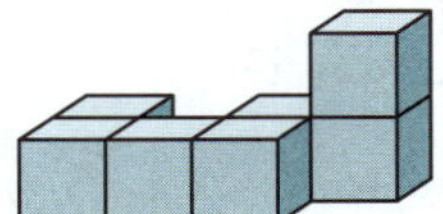

   What is the volume of the shape? .... cm³

5. 52 m² of fabric is used to make 13 identical shirts. How much fabric is used to make 5 shirts? .... m²

6. Find the mean of the first five odd numbers. ....

7. 172 500 people live in Higby. 100 times fewer people live in Borton than Higby. How many people live in Borton? ....

8. What is $\frac{7}{20}$ as a percentage? .... %

9. A sequence has the rule "add 9 to the previous term". The third term is 60. What is the first term? ....

10. The angles on the right make a right angle. What is the value of p? .... °

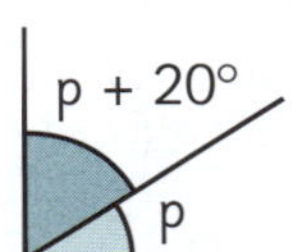

11. Work out $\frac{6}{7} \div 4$, giving your answer in its simplest form. ....

12. The size, x, of an exterior angle of a regular polygon with s sides is given by $x = \frac{360°}{s}$. How many sides does a regular polygon with exterior angles of 60° have? ....

Part B

13. Use the conversion 5 miles ≈ 8 km to convert 100 miles into km. .... km

14. At a cafe, 32% of customers order tea, $\frac{7}{25}$ order coffee and the rest order water. What percentage of the customers order water? .... %

15. What is 5 × 1.16? ....

16. Francis earns £10.50 an hour. How much does he earn in 6 hours? £ ....

17. Rick's garden is shown on the diagram below. He wants to put a fence around the edge. How many metres of fence will he need?

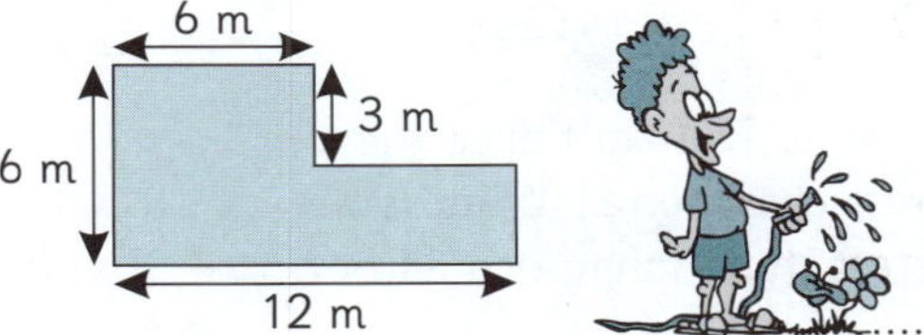

.... m

18. Work out 176 500 + 80 025. ....

19. Theo's bag weighs 24.5 kg. Amy's bag weighs 26.3 kg. How much more does Amy's bag weigh than Theo's? .... kg

20. Work out $\frac{3}{5} \times \frac{1}{4}$. ....

21. This pie chart shows how Wes spent £180 on clothes, food and travel. How much more did he spend on travel than on food?

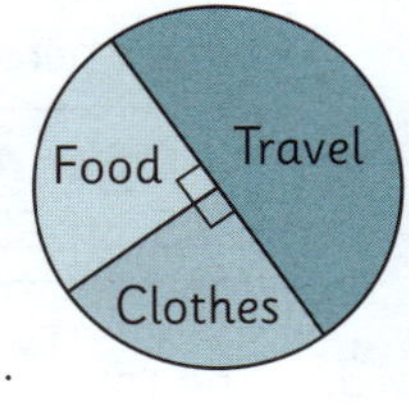

£ ....

22. A triangle has an area of 60 m². It has a vertical height of 10 m. How long is its base? .... m

23. What is $3\frac{3}{4} + 1\frac{3}{8}$? ....

24. How many factors of 24 are prime? ....

© CGP — not to be photocopied

Test 4

Part A

1. What is 1.550 litres + 25 ml in litres? l

2. What is 4% of 500? ....

3. A hotel serves 956 eggs on Saturday and 830 eggs on Sunday. How many more eggs were served on Saturday? ....

4. What is $\frac{2}{5} + \frac{3}{10} + \frac{1}{20}$ in its simplest form? ....

5. This pie chart shows the hair colours of the 36 members of a choir. How many members have grey hair?

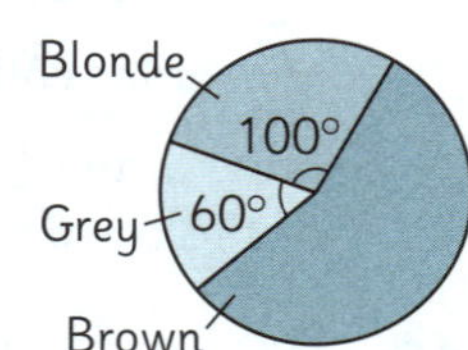

....

6. A triangle has an area of 24 cm². The base of the triangle is 8 cm long. What is the height of the triangle? .... cm

7. What is the missing number in this sequence?

64, 78, ⎡?⎤, 106, 120 ....

8. Hannah is 154 cm tall to the nearest centimetre. What is the shortest that Hannah could be? .... cm

9. What is −135 + 210? ....

10. A parallelogram has an area of 36 cm². Its vertical height is 9 cm. What is the length of its base? .... cm

11. A bottle holds 1.15 litres of water. How much would 4 bottles hold? l

12. Which offer below gives a bigger percentage discount?

Offer A	**Offer B**
£5 off £50	£3 off £20

....

13. The ratio of red to blue pens is 5 : 4. There are 20 blue pens. How many red pens are there? ....

14. What is 3600 ÷ 40? ....

15. A batch of cookies uses $\frac{3}{4}$ kg of sugar. How much sugar would be needed to make half of a batch of cookies? .... kg

Part B

16. Which is smaller: $\frac{17}{25}$ or 64%? ....

17. The mean number of spots on ten ladybirds is 4.3. What is the total number of spots on the ladybirds? ....

18. Deb raised £920 for charity. Ross raised 3 times as much as Deb. How much did they raise in total? £ ....

19. What is the remainder when 308 is divided by 6? ....

20. Use the conversion 5 miles ≈ 8 km to convert 48 km to miles. .... miles

21. $4 + 2 \times 6 = 8 \times (\boxed{?} - 5)$
What is the missing number? ....

22. A box of pencils is 10 cm tall, 2 cm wide and 20 cm long. What is the volume of the box of pencils? .... cm³

23. Tilly runs $2\frac{3}{4}$ km. Lyle runs $1\frac{5}{8}$ km. How many kilometres further does Tilly run than Lyle as a mixed number? .... km

24. What is the size of angle x in this isosceles triangle?

....

25. Which is the biggest volume: 1.938 litres, 1928 ml or 1958 ml? ....

26. Three angles in a quadrilateral are 75°, 115° and 60°. What is the size of the fourth angle? .... °

27. Look at the formula V = LWH. What is the value of V when L = 3, W = 2 and H = 4? ....

28. What is $4\frac{2}{3} \times 4$ as a mixed number in its simplest form? ....

29. 328 people went to a football game by minibus. Minibuses seat 8 passengers. How many minibuses did they need? ....

30. $3q + 4 = 2q + 6$
What is the value of q? ....

© CGP — not to be photocopied

Test 5

Part A

1. Round 5995 to the nearest ten. ....

2. Which of these amounts is the smallest?

   | 0.64 | $\frac{2}{3}$ | 65% |

   ....

3. What is 600×120? ....

4. A parallelogram has a base of 12 cm and a vertical height of 4 cm. What is the area of the parallelogram? .... cm^2

5. A pack contains 6 cans of fizzy drink. Lydia buys 15 packs, then gives 27 cans away. How many cans of fizzy drink does she have left? ....

6. $2 \times \bigcirc - 8 = 40$
   What is the value of $\bigcirc$? ....

7. A cube has a side length of 3 mm. What is the volume of the cube? .... mm^3

8. What is $\frac{1}{2} \times \frac{1}{8}$? ....

9. The rule for a sequence is "add 4". The first term is 3. What is the 100th term? ....

10. This shape is a parallelogram. What is the size of angle q? 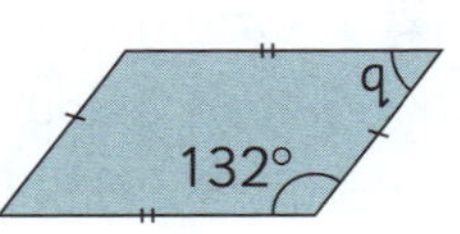

    ....°

11. Quinn reads $\frac{3}{10}$ of the pages in her book on Monday and 25% on Tuesday. What fraction does she have left to read in its simplest form? ....

12. What is 5×2.15? ....

13. Kate has 15 rock albums for every 30 pop albums. She has 90 pop albums. How many rock albums does she have? ....

14. Find the largest number that is a factor of both 77 and 110. ....

15. A square has an area of 49 mm^2. What is the perimeter of the square? .... mm

Part B

16. A pie chart shows the results of a survey taken by 60 people. What angle on the pie chart represents one person? ....°

17. Find $\frac{13}{20}$ of 200. ....

18. Ryan has 1.35 litres of orange squash. 120 ml of squash is needed per serving. How many servings can he make? ....

19. A submarine is at −450 m. The ocean floor is at −800 m. What is the difference between them in kilometres? .... km

20. What is $\frac{9}{10} \div 6$ in its simplest form? ....

21. What is the size of angle e? ....° 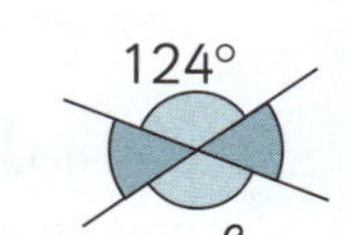

22. Five apples have a mean mass of 100 g. An orange is added, and the mean mass of all the fruit is now 110 g. What is the mass of the orange? .... g

23. What is the sixth term in the sequence with the rule $2n - 5$? ....

24. A bag contains 120 marbles, 24 of which are green. What percentage of the marbles are green? .... %

25. What is 3760 g − 1.05 kg in grams? .... g

26. Jo runs 20 laps of a running track. The track is 380 m long. How far does she run? .... m

27. What is the area of the triangle on the right? .... cm^2 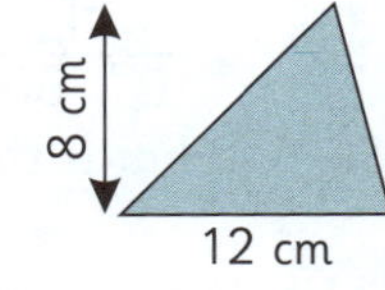

28. Work out $\frac{11}{7} + 1\frac{5}{7}$, giving your answer as a mixed number. ....

29. Skirts usually cost £20, but they are 30% off in a sale. How much would it cost to buy three skirts in the sale? £..................

30. $421 - (\boxed{?} \div 12) = 409$
    What is the missing number? ....

© CGP — not to be photocopied

Test 6

Warm Up Questions

Three out of every seven animals on a farm are sheep. There are 240 sheep on the farm.

1) What is the ratio of sheep to other animals on the farm in its simplest form?

2) How many animals on the farm aren't sheep?

Part A

1. What is $3.79 \div 10$? ....

2. How many hours are in 1.5 days? .... hours

3. What is $9650 - 4080$? ....

4. Work out $\frac{5}{6} \times \frac{1}{10}$, giving your answer in its simplest form. ....

5. Liz cycles 32 km. Approximately how many miles does she cycle? Use the conversion 5 miles ≈ 8 km. .... miles

6. What is the size of angle m? .... °

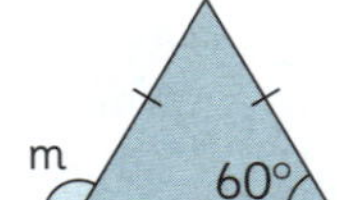

7. A cafe sells cups of tea for £1 and cookies for £1.50. How much money do they get in total from 70 cups of tea and 100 cookies? £ ....

8. What is 7×250? ....

9. A sink contains 5.7 litres of water. 850 ml of water is added. How many ml of water are now in the sink? .... ml

10. $2\frac{1}{10} + \dfrac{\boxed{?}}{30} = \dfrac{91}{30}$

What is the missing number? ....

11. What is the area of the parallelogram that has a base of 6 cm and a vertical height of 5 cm? .... cm^2

12. What is seven hundred and six minus three hundred and fifty-eight? ....

13. Sandy and Will share 63 g of popping candy in the ratio 4:3. How much more does Sandy get than Will? .... g

Part B

14. What is $\dfrac{64}{400}$ as a decimal? ....

15. A sequence has the rule "subtract 4 from the previous term". The third term is 7. What is the first term? ....

16. Find the smallest number that is a multiple of 4, 10 and 25. ....

17. What is the size of angle k? .... °

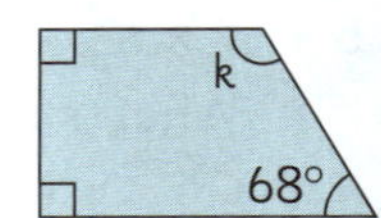

18. The distance around the Sun is 4 378 993 km. Round this to the nearest hundred thousand km. .... km

19. A cuboid box has a volume of 120 cm^3. It is 10 cm long and 3 cm tall. What is the width of the box? .... cm

20. $\frac{1}{4}$ of pupils in Rina's class have a dog. 6 pupils have a dog. How many pupils are in Rina's class? ....

21. $c = 5 + 4a - b$. What is the value of c if a = 5 and b = 2? ....

22. Shape A below is enlarged to give shape B. What is the scale factor of the enlargement?

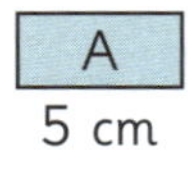
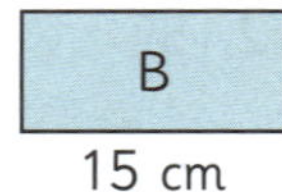

5 cm   15 cm ....

23. $\boxed{?} + 63 \div 7 = 83$

What is the missing number? ....

24. A pie chart shows how 120 people travelled to work. 30 people travelled by train. What angle should the 'train' sector be on the pie chart? .... °

  © CGP — not to be photocopied

Test 7

Part A

1. Work out 246 285 − 30 200. ....

2. Betty walks 12.87 km. How far does she walk to the nearest hundred metres? .... m

3. What is $\frac{14}{40}$ as a percentage? .... %

4. The nth term of a sequence is 2n + 9. What is the 5th term? ....

5. What is the size of angle p? .... °

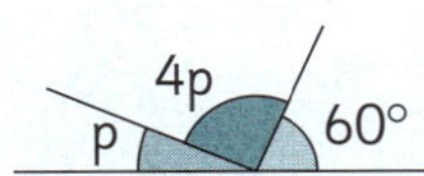

6. A cuboid is 5 cm long, 4 cm wide and 2 cm high. What is its volume? .... cm³

7. 5x − 3 = 12 What is the value of x? ....

8. A tub of ice cream weighs 720 g. Trey buys 4 tubs, then eats 300 g. How much does he have left? .... g

9. 6 × (81 ÷ ⬚) = 54 What is the missing number? ....

10. The size, x, of an angle inside a regular polygon with s sides is given by x = 180° − $\frac{360°}{s}$. What is the size of an angle inside a regular hexagon? .... °

11. 10 school uniforms cost £280. What would 3 school uniforms cost? £ ....

12. A triathlete swims 800 m, cycles 2.4 km and runs 6000 m. How many km do they complete in total? .... km

13. Two angles in a triangle are 50° and 72°. What is the size of the third angle? .... °

14. A computer is sold for 30% off. Its original price was £600. What is its price now?

£ ....

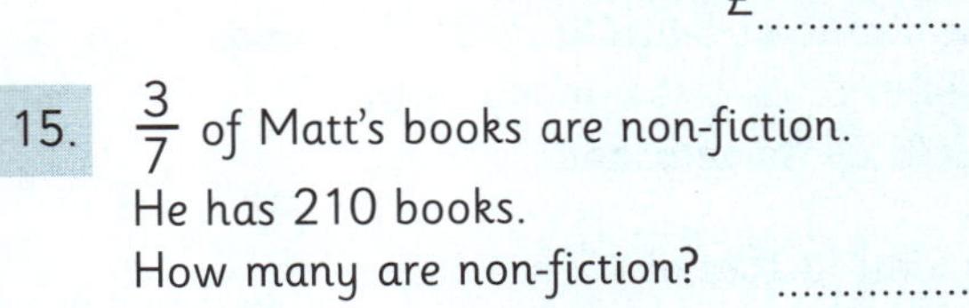

15. $\frac{3}{7}$ of Matt's books are non-fiction. He has 210 books. How many are non-fiction? ....

Part B

16. A bag of crisps weighs 25.08 g. How much do 12 bags weigh? .... g

17. This triangle has an area of 30 m². What is the value of h? .... m

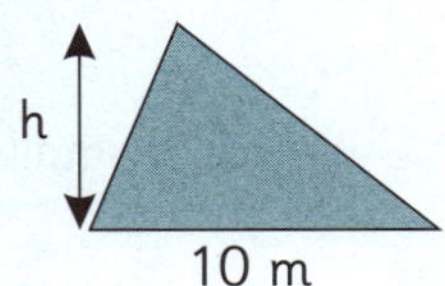

18. Samira and Jill baked some cakes in the ratio 5 : 4. They baked 54 cakes in total. How many cakes did Samira bake? ....

19. Abi's bank balance was −£320. She got paid £1570. What was her bank balance after getting paid? £ ....

20. What is $\frac{8}{12} ÷ 4$ in its simplest form? ....

21. What is 624 ÷ 12, rounded to the nearest ten? ....

22. Bob has $1\frac{1}{10}$ kg of apples. He uses $\frac{2}{5}$ kg. How many kg of apples are left? .... kg

23. The area of a parallelogram is 6 mm². Its vertical height is 4 mm. What is its width? .... mm

24. 1548 + ⬚ = 1752 What is the missing number? ....

25. This pie chart shows the types of biscuits in a box. There are 15 plain biscuits in the box. How many biscuits are in the box in total? ....

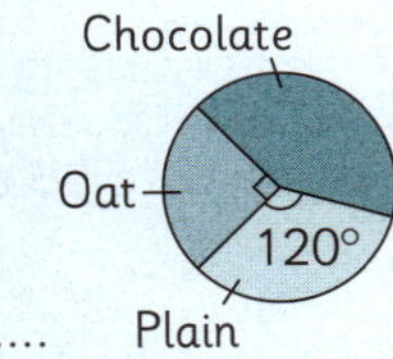

26. Find the mean of 1.3, 1.7 and 2.4. ....

27. Helen walked 4 km. Ted walked 3 miles. How much further did Ted walk in miles? Use the conversion 5 miles ≈ 8 km. .... miles

28. What is 0.24 as a fraction in its simplest form? ....

29. Naysha's house is 612 m from the park. She walks from her house to the park and back twice. How far is that in total? .... m

30. Which is a smaller amount: 5.007 kg or 5070 g? ....

© CGP — not to be photocopied

Test 8

Part A

1. Lia wins £25 000 to the nearest £5000. What is the largest whole number of pounds she could have won?   £ ....

2. Which is smaller: 1.57 or $1\frac{3}{5}$?   ....

3. Use the conversion 5 miles ≈ 8 km to convert 8.8 km into miles.   .... miles

4. $\frac{d}{5} + 1 = 3$
   What is the value of d?   ....

5. An apple tree is 480 cm tall. A pear tree is 1750 mm tall. How many cm smaller than the apple tree is the pear tree?   .... cm

6. $\frac{1}{2}$ of a red pencil and $\frac{1}{3}$ of a yellow pencil are the same length. The red pencil is 10 cm long. How long is the yellow pencil?   .... cm

7. What is $4 \times (7 + 1) + 14$?   ....

8. Amara has 125 blocks. She loses 17, then splits the rest into 4 equal piles. How many blocks are in each pile?   ....

9. What is the size of the missing angle in this quadrilateral?   ....°

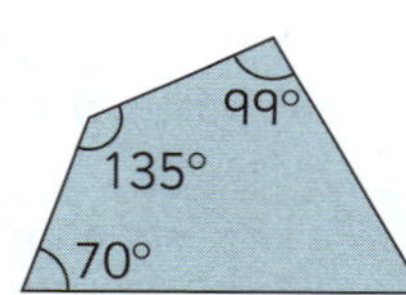

10. Write 68 days in weeks and days.   .... weeks .... days

11. $510\ 010 + \boxed{?} = 1\ 310\ 100$
    What is the missing number?   ....

12. What is $0.56 \div 7$?   ....

13. The formula for the time, T, to cook a piece of beef weighing W kg, in minutes, is $T = 30W + 20$. How long does it take to cook a 3 kg piece of beef?   .... mins

14. What is the mean of 9 °C, 16 °C, 7 °C and 12 °C?   .... °C

15. A bakery makes 348 cookies. They sell 289. How many are left?   ....

Part B

16. What is $27\ 500 + 80\ 000$?   ....

17. Wendy runs $3\frac{1}{2}$ km. Adam runs $5\frac{3}{16}$ km. How many km do they run in total?   .... km

18. Find the area of this triangle.

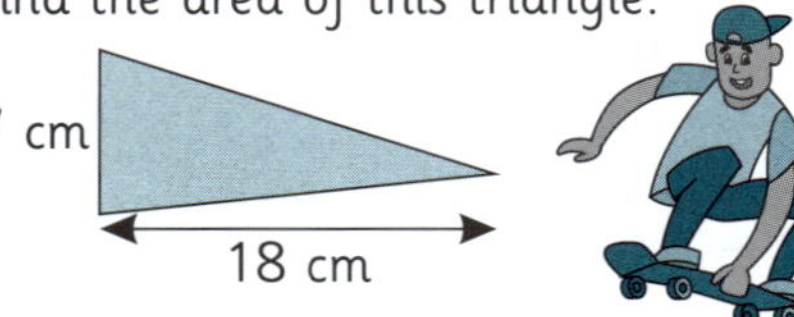

   .... cm²

19. What is one quarter multiplied by two fifths in its simplest form?   ....

20. A belt costs £25. It is reduced by £6 in a sale. What percentage discount is this?   .... %

21. Work out 18.12×1000.   ....

22. Two angles added together make a right angle. One of the angles is 37°. What is the other angle?   ....°

23. $\frac{5}{10}$ of $\boxed{?} = 20$
    What is the missing number?   ....

24. The area of a parallelogram is 108 mm². It is 12 mm wide. What is its vertical height?   .... mm

25. What is 45% of 120?   ....

26. The volume of a cuboid-shaped room is 120 m³. It is 6 m long and 4 m high. What is the width of the room?   .... m

27. A sequence begins 9, 5, 1, ... What is the 5th term of the sequence?   ....

28. This pie chart shows the ingredients in a 30 g portion of muesli. How many more grams of oats are there than raisins?   .... g

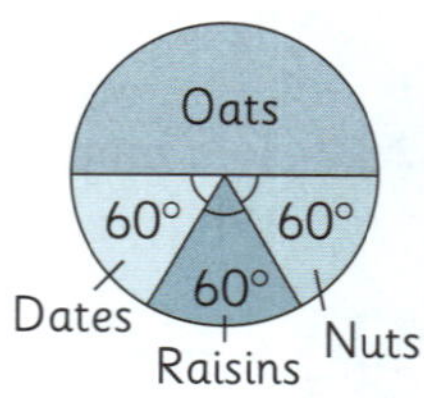

29. The ratio of bags of gravel to bags of sand sold at a garden centre is 8 : 3. 110 bags are sold in total. How many of the bags sold contained sand?   ....

30. How many factors of 42 are prime?   ....

© CGP — not to be photocopied

Test 9

Part A

1. What is 40 000 − 4250? ....

2. Convert 15.14 mm to cm. .... cm

3. What is 52% of 400? ....

4. Rylan spills $\frac{3}{20}$ of a bottle of cola and pours 20% of the original amount into a glass. What fraction of the cola is left in the bottle in its simplest form? ....

5. What is the area of this triangle?

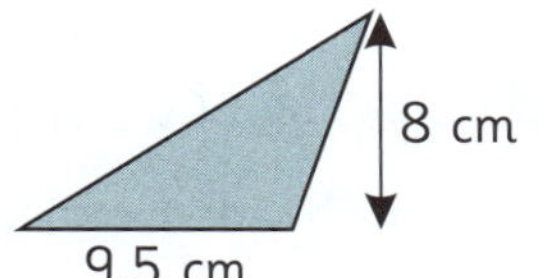

.... cm²

6. Work out 7.2 ÷ 4. ....

7. A sequence has the rule "subtract 8". The third term of the sequence is 6. What is the first term? ....

8. List the digits that could go in the box to make this statement correct:

6 707 8 $\boxed{?}$ 9 < 6 707 820 ....

9. Use the conversion 5 miles ≈ 8 km to convert 35 miles into kilometres. .... km

10. A jug can hold 4.15 litres of water. How much water can 3 jugs hold? l

11. The size, x, of an exterior angle of a regular polygon with s sides is given by $x = \frac{360°}{s}$. What is the size of an exterior angle of a regular octagon? .... °

12. x = 1 and y = 4 satisfies the equation 3x + y = 7. What other pair of positive whole numbers satisfy this equation?

x = ..., y = ...

13. What is 50 ÷ 5 × 5? ....

14. 90 people are surveyed about their favourite shop. Their answers are shown on a pie chart. What angle represents each person on the pie chart? .... °

15. What is the size of angle k in the triangle on the right?

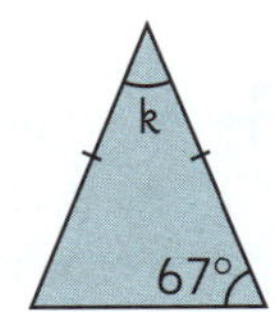

.... °

Part B

16. The mean number of sweets in three bags is 9. There are 10 sweets in the first bag and 7 sweets in the second bag. How many are in the third bag? ....

17. A library has 8824 books, split equally across 8 shelves. How many books are on each shelf? ....

18. What is −73 − 15? ....

19. Two angles in a quadrilateral are 83° and the third angle is 114°. What is the size of the fourth angle? .... °

20. Look at the formula m = 3n + 1. What is the value of m when n = 4? ....

21. 983 + 147 − $\boxed{?}$ = 1000 What is the missing number? ....

22. A parallelogram has a base of 15 mm and a vertical height of 8 mm. What is the area of the parallelogram? .... mm²

23. What is $\frac{7}{8} + 1\frac{1}{4}$ as a mixed number? ....

24. Which number between 110 and 130 is a common multiple of 8 and 12? ....

25. This cuboid has a volume of 60 cm³. What is the length of side x?

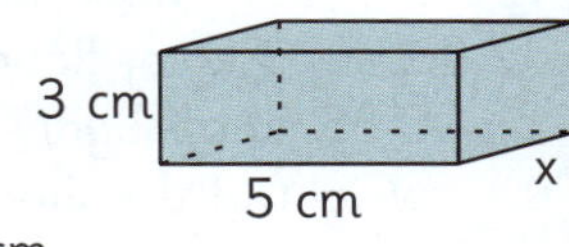

.... cm

26. What is $\frac{7}{15}$ of 45? ....

27. In a car park, there are 8 red cars for every 5 blue cars. There are 96 red cars. How many blue cars are there? ....

28. Work out 6314 ÷ 7. ....

29. A shape is 4 cm long. After it is enlarged, it is 16 cm long. What was the scale factor of the enlargement? ....

30. 1.5 litres of water and 150 ml of bleach are mixed to make a cleaning product. How many ml of product are made? .... ml

© CGP — not to be photocopied

Section Three

Test 10

Warm Up Questions

1) Poppy has one quarter of a pizza. She cuts the quarter into 4 equal slices.
   What fraction of the whole pizza is each slice?

2) What is $\frac{1}{5} \div 4$ in its simplest form?

Part A

1. What is 0.81×5? ....

2. Round 4 075 407 to the nearest ten thousand. ....

3. Write 72% as a fraction in its simplest form. ....

4. What is the highest common factor of 18, 24 and 60? ....

5. Faye runs 9 miles a day. How many kilometres will she run in 5 days?
    Use the conversion 5 miles ≈ 8 km. .... km

6. Shape B is an enlargement of Shape A.
    What is the length of the side x?

    .... m

7. A baker makes shortbread dough using 3 kg of flour, 1500 g butter and
    0.75 kg of sugar. What is the total weight of the shortbread dough in g? .... g

8. Calculate $1217 + 834$. ....

9. Harry sells 100 posters, each for the same price. They sell for £499 in total.
    How much did each poster sell for? £....................

10. Look at the formula $v = u + at$.
    What is the value of u when
    $v = 12$, $a = 2$ and $t = 4$? ....

11. How many minutes are in $5\frac{4}{5}$ hours? .... mins

12. Which is the smaller percentage discount? A: £650 off £1000
    or B: £350 off £500. ....

Part B

13. $607\ 200 + \boxed{?} = 812\ 200$
    What is the missing number? ....

14. 400 ml of water fills $\frac{1}{6}$ of a flask. How
    much water can the flask hold in ml? .... ml

15. What is the volume of this cuboid?

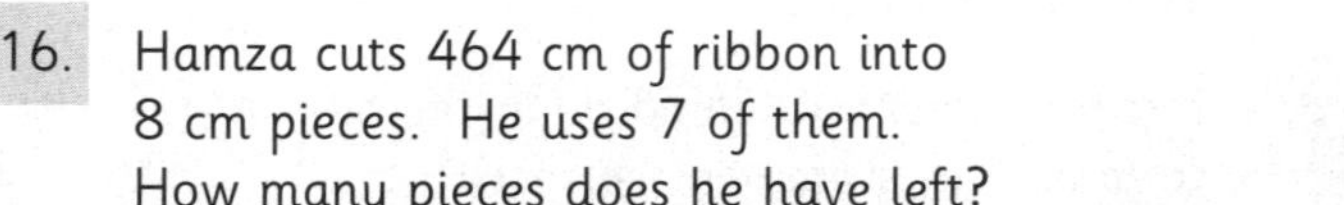

    .... mm³

16. Hamza cuts 464 cm of ribbon into
    8 cm pieces. He uses 7 of them.
    How many pieces does he have left? ....

17. What is $150 \div (17 + 8)$? ....

18. What is the third term in the sequence with first term 3
    and rule "subtract 0.5"? ....

19. What is $\frac{3}{8} - \frac{1}{3}$? ....

20. The mean score on a test was 7.
    21 pupils took the test.
    What was the total number
    of marks on all the tests? ....

21. What is $33\ 000 \div 11$? ....

22. $\frac{4}{5}$ of Mel's toy cars are red. She shares
    the red cars equally between six boxes.
    What fraction of Mel's cars is
    in each box, in its simplest form? ....

23. What is the size of angle g? ....°

24. A triangle has an area of 160 cm².
    Its vertical height is 20 cm.
    What is the width of its base? .... cm

© CGP — not to be photocopied

Test 11

Part A

1. What is 2834 − 622? ....

2. Which of these is the biggest: $\frac{21}{25}$, 0.83 or 85%? ....

3. What is 278.9 ÷ 100? ....

4. 36 people picked their favourite sauce. 10 people chose ketchup. What angle would represent this on a pie chart? .... °

5. What is the size of angle p? .... ° 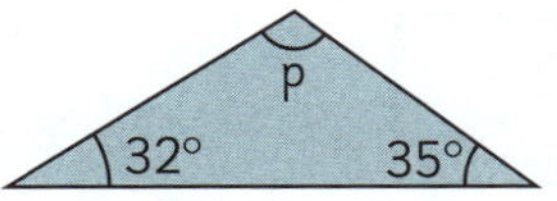

6. What is $\frac{2}{3} \times 36$? ....

7. The temperature in a shed at 6 am was −5 °C. At 3 pm, it had risen by 8.5 °C. What was the temperature in the shed at 3 pm? .... °C

8. What is 360 g + 10.52 kg in grams? .... g

9. Three angles meet around a point. Two of the angles are 127° and 28°. What is the third angle? .... °

10. A farmer has two pigs. One eats 2.6 kg of food a day and the other eats 2450 g. How many kg of food do the pigs eat in total each day? .... kg

11. Work out $\frac{11}{6} - \frac{1}{5}$. ....

12. This shape is made out of 5 cm³ cubes. What is the volume of the shape? .... cm³ 

13. Janet makes 226 cards and Olly makes 194 cards. How many cards do they make in total? ....

14. Find the missing number in this sequence: [?], −18, −11, −4, ...

15. A hotel has 16 rooms that sleep 2 people, and 12 rooms that sleep 4 people. What is the maximum number of people that can stay at the hotel at once? ....

Part B

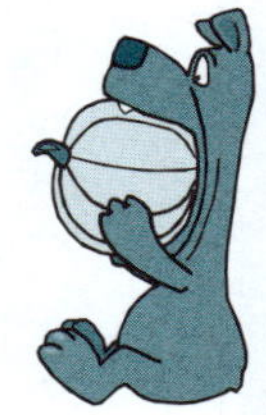

16. Three pumpkins weigh 12.5 kg, 9.5 kg and 8 kg. What is the mean weight of the three pumpkins? .... kg

17. A triangle has a base of 7 cm and a vertical height of 12 cm. What is the area of the triangle? .... cm²

18. $(69 - 5) \div$ [?] $+ 3 = 11$ What is the missing number? ....

19. What is 145 multiplied by 6? ....

20. Kwame drives 48 km to work. How far does he drive in miles? Use the conversion 5 miles ≈ 8 km. .... miles

21. What is 9% of 80? ....

22. In a bowl of peanuts and cashew nuts, there are 6 cashew nuts for every 14 peanuts. There are 80 nuts in the bowl. How many peanuts are there? ....

23. $7 + 2 \times$ [ ] $= 19$ What is the value of [ ]? ....

24. A textbook costs £6.99. Mr Jones buys 7 textbooks. What is the total cost? £ ....

25. Round the answer to 219 × 3 to the nearest hundred. ....

26. The formula $C = 5 + 3p$ gives the cost £C of hiring a boat for p people. Jacob spends £23 hiring a boat. How many people was it for? ....

27. Four bags of icing sugar cost £3.60. How much are 7 bags of icing sugar? £ ....

28. What is $1\frac{3}{10} + \frac{7}{20}$? ....

29. What is the area of this parallelogram? .... m² 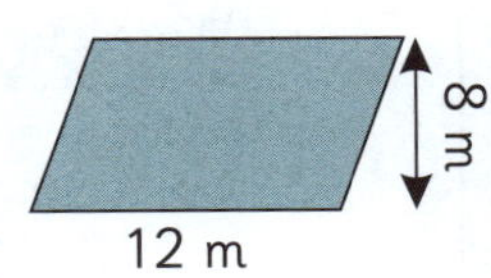

30. A plank of wood is $\frac{3}{5}$ m long. It is cut into 4 equal lengths. How long is each piece? .... m

© CGP — not to be photocopied

Section Three

Section 3 Progress Test

1) The average daily temperature in Sproxby in August is 21 °C higher than it is in January. In January, the average daily temperature is −5 °C.

What is the average daily temperature in August?

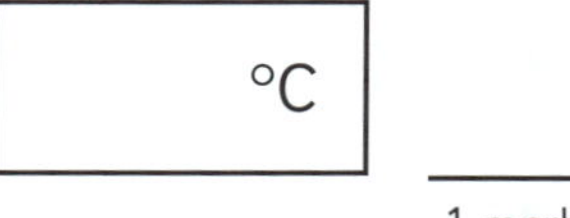

°C

1 mark

2) Fill in the missing numbers in these calculations.

$$152 \times 6 = \boxed{}$$

1 mark

$$7082 - \boxed{} = 2550$$

1 mark

3) Jackie says, "If you add 15 to my age in years, and then divide it by 6, you get 4."

How old is Jackie?

1 mark

4) The patio in a garden is shown in the diagram on the right.

What is the area of the patio?

m²

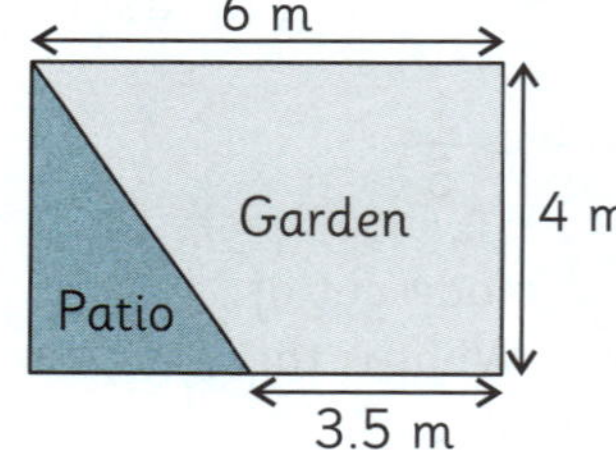

1 mark

5) Work out these fraction calculations, giving your answers as mixed numbers.

$$1\frac{7}{12} + \frac{5}{6} = \boxed{} \qquad \frac{7}{3} - \frac{4}{9} = \boxed{}$$

2 marks

© CGP — not to be photocopied

Section 3 Progress Test

6) Fill in the missing numbers in this sequence.

8 | [ ] | 11 | 12.5 | [ ] | 15.5

2 marks

7) Tina makes bunches of flowers. This pie chart shows how many of each type of flower she uses in each bunch.

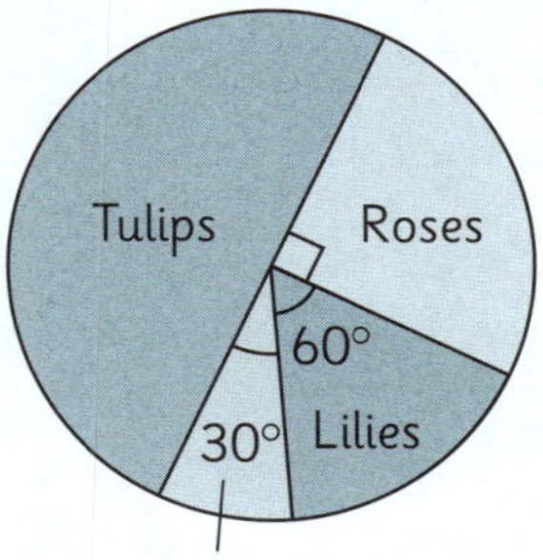

What fraction of the flowers in each bunch are sunflowers?

1 mark

Each bunch has 24 flowers in it. How many lilies are in a bunch?

1 mark

8) A roll holds 12.5 m of wire. Christian cuts 30 pieces of wire from it. Each piece is 40 cm long.

How many metres of wire are left on the roll?

m

1 mark

He uses 40% of the pieces of wire to make a sculpture. How many pieces does he have left?

1 mark

9) Look at the quadrilateral shown on the right.

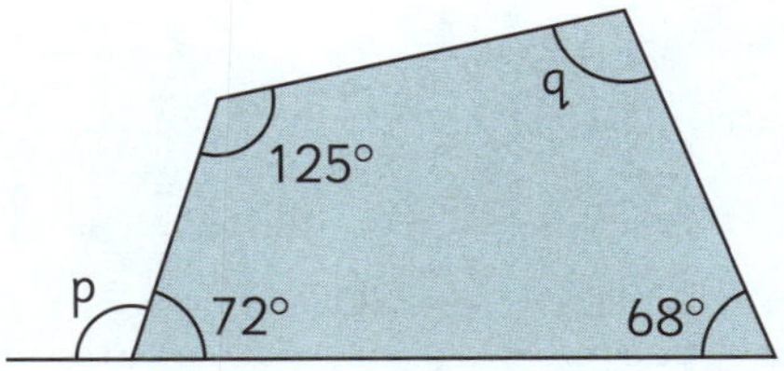

What is the size of angle p?

°

1 mark

What is the size of angle q?

°

1 mark

© CGP — not to be photocopied

Section 3 Listening Tests

Go to cgpbooks.co.uk/MA-Year6 or scan the QR code on the right to find the audio files for these listening tests. Listen carefully to each question before writing down your answer in the spaces provided for each test.

Each test has ten questions. You will have 5 seconds to answer each of the first five questions, and 10 seconds to answer each of the last five questions.

Listening Test 1

1. ....

2. .... %

3. ....

4. ....

5. ....

6. .... ml

7. ....

8. £ ....

9. ....

10. ....

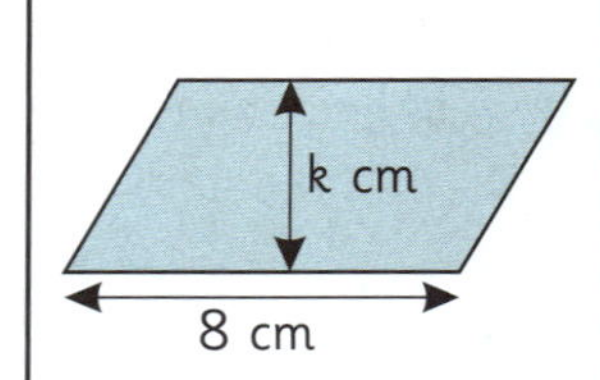

Listening Test 2

1. .... mm

2. ....

3. ....

4. ....

5. ....

6. .... °

7. .... kg

8. ....

9. £ ....

10. .... g

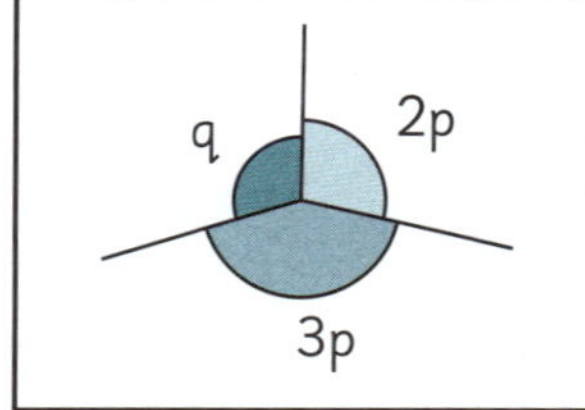

Listening Test 3

1. ....

2. ....

3. ....

4. .... km

5. ....

6. .... °

7. ....

8. £ ....

9. .... cm

10. ....

© CGP — not to be photocopied

M6AQ21